Glory

Douglas Dales is Chaplain and Head of RE at Marlborough College, Wiltshire. A Fellow of the Royal Historical Society, he is the author of *Dunstan – Saint and Statesman*, *Light to the Isles*, *Living Through Dying* (all published by Lutterworth) and *Called to Be Angels – An Introduction to Anglo-Saxon Spirituality*, *Christ the Golden Blossom* and *This Is My Faith* (published by the Canterbury Press).

Glory

The Spiritual Theology of Michael Ramsey

Douglas Dales

CANTERBURY
PRESS
Norwich

© Douglas Dales 2003

First published in 2003 by the Canterbury Press Norwich
(a publishing imprint of Hymns Ancient & Modern Limited,
a registered charity)
St Mary's Works, St Mary's Plain,
Norwich, Norfolk, NR3 3BH

www.scm-canterburypress.co.uk

British Cataloguing in Publication data

A catalogue record for this book is available
from the British Library

Bible quotations are generally taken from
The Revised English Bible
© Oxford and Cambridge University Press

ISBN 1-85311-535-5

Typeset by Regent Typesetting, London
Printed and bound by
Biddles Ltd, www.biddles.co.uk

The Glory of God is the living man;
And the life of man is the Vision of God.

+

Dedicated with gratitude to
the Sisters of the Love of God

Contents

Contents

Acknowledgements

Sincere thanks are due to the Sisters of the Love of God for permission to quote from *The Christian Concept of Sacrifice* by Michael Ramsey, and from their other publications as attributed; to the Friends of York Minster for permission to use adapted extracts from *My God, My Glory* by Eric Milner-White; and to SPCK for permission to quote from *The Gospel and the Catholic Church*, *The Christian Priest Today*, and *The Holy Spirit*, all by Michael Ramsey. It has not been possible to trace permissions to quote from Michael Ramsey's other published works, all of which are now out of print, but all quotations are fully attributed.

Preface

I had the good fortune to meet Michael Ramsey as he retired from being Archbishop of Canterbury in 1974, and came to Cuddesdon, near Oxford, where I was training to become a priest in the Church of England. Circumstances and common interests rather threw us together, and out of it a firm friendship was born, which lasted until his death in Oxford in April 1988. Bishop Michael, as he liked to be called, and his wife, Lady Ramsey, showed every kindness to my wife and me, and in due time to our children as well, on our visits to them in Durham and Oxford. This is therefore the portrait of a friend, as well as a study and exposition of the spiritual theology of the 100th Archbishop of Canterbury; and that is why he is referred to as 'Bishop Michael' throughout the main part of this book.

He was a wonderful teacher and spiritual mentor, with a most alert mind, hilarious wit, and an eager spirit of interest and enquiry. To visit him was to be welcomed by warmth and silence in equal measure. To speak to him in person or by telephone was to sense immediately his kindness and total interest. His greatest gift was to encourage and to impart a sense of joy, which dispelled despondency and any narrowness of vision. Even in the memory this remains potent and true; he fulfilled his own dictum about being a saint – he made God real.

Memory is a powerful thing, and Bishop Michael certainly leaves a lively sense of his presence and character upon it. Many of our conversations occurred walking through the fields around Cuddesdon, or along the river in Durham. There were extraordinary moments such as when he got stuck on a stile and refused to move until he had finished what he was saying; or when he fell into a snow-drift in Durham and lay there laughing and throwing snowballs, and then got up covered in snow to make a point about theology!

He was generous with his time and with his books, never happier than when he could get on with whatever was in hand, while a young student sat lodged in the corner of his study with a volume of the Fathers. He would pace up and down, and then suddenly ask what one was reading and make a pertinent or ironic comment about it, before lapsing back into purposeful silence. He taught as much by his silences as by his words, by his attitude and example as by his advice, which he was often cautious about giving. He was a loving father-in-God, as well as, in the words placed on his memorial at Canterbury Cathedral, a 'scholar, priest and friend'.

I am grateful to all those who have encouraged this study, and especially to Bishop Peter Walker, Sister Benedicta Ward and Sister Isabel Mary; also to Fathers Emmanuele Bargellini and Innocenzo Gargano of Camaldoli and Rome, and Father Yves Dubois, Orthodox priest in Bath. My colleagues, the Revd James Dickie and the Revd Canon Henry Pearson, have been of real encouragement too, as have the Master of Marlborough College and the Bishops of Salisbury and Ramsbury. Thanks must also go to Mrs Christine Smith for her wise help and advice in the publication of this book.

I am grateful also to my many pupils and confirmation candidates over 25 years, whose kindness, interest and perceptive questions have taught me so much about the meaning of Christianity. Finally, I must thank my dear wife, Geraldine, whose patience and good sense have rescued me from distractions and infelicities in the text; and also our children, Christopher, Gwendoline and Basil, for their good-natured support, and cheerful help with the mysteries of the computer!

Douglas Dales, Marlborough
The Feast of the Transfiguration, 2002

The prayers which preface each chapter are drawn from My God, My Glory, *by Eric Milner-White, formerly Dean of York.*

Introduction

This book is a study and an exposition of the spiritual theology of Michael Ramsey, as it is found in the printed books that he wrote over 50 years of ministry as a Christian priest and bishop within the Church of England. Other occasional writings also remain, mainly unpublished, but this book is restricted to using the published books, which represent his most considered thought, and his consistent attempt to make the heart of Christian faith and prayer accessible to a wide readership in the Church and beyond. This book is also intended to commemorate the centenary of his birth on 14 November 1904.

In his biography of Michael Ramsey, Owen Chadwick rightly observes that 'the best of him is to be found in extracts ... in the soul ruminating and thinking about the impact of Christ upon the world, and upon the guidance of God and the prayerful life'. He also observes how Michael Ramsey was brilliantly able 'to sum up a body of thinking in some telling phrase, with an insight that he could usually make clear to the simplest person'. As a result 'the certainty in his faith could be felt even by many who did not know him well. His sense of immediacy in God could be felt especially by those who came to know him well' (pp 373–4). The preparation of this book has certainly vindicated these judgements by someone who knew him closely, and whose biography remains the indispensable and authentic record of a remarkable life.

Now that almost all of Michael Ramsey's books are out of print, this book includes a significant number of quotations directly from his writings, in order that his voice might be heard again by those who remember him, and perhaps for the first time by a new generation of Christians in England and abroad. It is not simply a retrospective account, however, although it is rooted in a historical approach, and it is closely documented to enable readers to locate and get inside his thought. He was of course writing for an earlier generation, and it has seldom proved possible to alter his language to a more inclusive style. This book is intended none the less to relate his teaching, example and experience to the challenges and needs facing the modern Church as it proclaims the gospel by word, prayer and deed to our society.

It is intended also to further the cause of Christian unity within Anglicanism and beyond it. This was always very close to Michael Ramsey's heart, and its reality was etched upon it in many ways and over many years because of his own upbringing, and his personal and sometimes disappointing engagements with ecumenical relationships between the churches. He was always of the view that evangelical, catholic and liberal belong together within the life of the Church of England, and that their unity and fulfilment is to be found in a sound understanding of the gospel, and a sincere common commitment to a life of prayer and service to others. This book is intended to reaffirm the essential unity, identity and vitality of Anglican Christianity throughout the world, and to strengthen the integrity of its life and witness as it enters a new century and millennium.

Michael Ramsey believed also in the spiritual reality of the unity underlying the various branches of the Church, if they believed the same gospel and creeds, and celebrated the Eucharist at the heart of their life. Just as the great seal of Mount Athos comprises four parts, each entrusted to different persons, who must agree together if the seal is to be used; so Catholic, Orthodox, Anglican and Protestant are each and together entrusted with the fullness of the gospel and the means of life in Christ.

Four quarters only come together, however, in the form of the Cross, and Michael Ramsey asserted in his first book and maintained throughout his ministry that Christians are only drawn together in Christ as they learn the meaning of 'living through dying', both individually and corporately. It is only on this basis that they are called and enabled to pray and act together, while preserving and entering more deeply into their own distinctive inheritances. Christ's own prayer for unity, 'May they all be one', lays this as an urgent duty upon every Christian, for in this way God brings salvation and healing to humanity. This book will therefore be of interest outside the Anglican Communion as well, and especially among Catholic and Orthodox Christians. For in his day, Michael Ramsey was regarded across the world as an outstanding Christian leader.

This book comprises a rich body of spiritual teaching about the life in Christ and the reality of the Holy Spirit. Michael Ramsey's teaching sprang from a lifetime of prayer, thought and pastoral care, rooted in long-established traditions within the Anglican Church and elsewhere. It is therefore part of the living inheritance of English-speaking Christianity, and this study is intended to serve as a resource for its witness now and in the future. Michael Ramsey was always self-effacing, and he kept no diaries. This book examines directly and indirectly what flowed out from his inner spiritual experience, which must remain for ever hidden and unknown.

It starts with his early formation as a young ordinand and priest, a formation that was both stable and traumatic at the same time. Using his first book, *The Gospel and the Catholic Church*, as a framework, this study progresses through the unfolding of his teaching and belief about the heart of Christianity, as his ministry, writing and prayer developed. The chapter titles are drawn from seminal phrases in this first book. The prayers, which preface each chapter, are drawn and adapted from *My God, My Glory*, compiled by one of Michael Ramsey's beloved spiritual mentors, Eric Milner-White, formerly Dean of York. The book concludes with a picture of how Michael Ramsey saw the Anglican Catholic tradition, one of the longest and most profound tap-roots of spirituality and thought within Anglicanism, and one to which he felt deeply indebted. The central theme of this book is that of his own life, example and teaching: the personal call of God to holiness through union with Christ, by the power of the Holy Spirit within the life of the Church.

To read this book is therefore to enter upon a pilgrim's progress into the riches of Christ and the mystery of the Church's inner life. Its preparation has been a searching and at times very moving experience, as Michael Ramsey's gifts of thought and expression can sometimes wound the heart with compunction. His style of writing is succinct and intense, and behind the clarity of his thought there is always a high charge of urgency and emotion. There is steel too, as the scalpel of the gospel never wavered or tarnished in his hand. His sense of the reality of God and of the depth of human need moved him with great conviction and compassion. He never lost the force of evangelical vision born of his own encounter with Christ, while at the same time imparting a sense of the mystery of God hidden within the catholic prayer and worship of the Church. Like St Anthony of old in the desert, he was a person of whom it could truly be said: 'To see you, father, is sufficient.'

Michael Ramsey
– A Biographical Outline

1904 Born in Cambridge on 14 November
1927 First-class degree in Theology at Cambridge; ordinand at Cuddesdon, Oxford
1928 Ordained as curate of St Nicholas, Liverpool
1930 Sub-Warden at Lincoln theological college
1936 Published *The Gospel and the Catholic Church*
1937 Senior curate at Boston, Lincolnshire
1939 Vicar of St Benet's, Cambridge
1940 Canon professor of theology at Durham
1942 Married to Joan Hamilton (Lady Ramsey)
1950 Regius professor of Divinity at Cambridge
1952 Bishop of Durham
1956 Archbishop of York
1961 Archbishop of Canterbury
1966 Meeting with Pope Paul VI in Rome
1974 Retired to Cuddesdon
1977 Moved to Durham
1986 Moved to Bishopthorpe, York
1987 Moved to St John's Home, Oxford
1988 Died on 23 April: buried at Canterbury Cathedral on 3 May
1995 Death of Lady Ramsey: buried at Canterbury Cathedral on 17 February

Part One:
The Meaning of the Cross

I

Living through Dying

O Lord Christ, Lamb of God, Lord of Lords,
Call us, who are called to be saints, along the way of thy Cross:
Draw us, who would draw nearer to our King, to the foot of
thy Cross:
Cleanse us, who are not worthy to approach, with the pardon
of thy Cross:
Instruct us, the ignorant and blind, in the school of thy Cross:
Arm us, for the battles of holiness, by the might of thy Cross:
Bring us, in the fellowship of thy sufferings, to the victory of
thy Cross:
Seal us in the kingdom of thy glory among the servants of thy
Cross:
O crucified Lord,
Who with the Father and the Holy Spirit
Livest and reignest one God, almighty, eternal, for ever.

*

Bishop Michael was a sensitive person whose priesthood was forged in a crucible of suffering. Shortly after his arrival to train as a priest at the theological college at Cuddesdon, near Oxford, in the summer of 1927, his mother died in a tragic road accident; and just before he had finished his first curacy in Liverpool, his revered elder brother died, early in 1930. Meanwhile as he was about to commit his life to the ministry of the Church of England, the House of Commons threw out its new prayer book in 1928. In the words of his biographer, Owen Chadwick, 'the resulting turmoil, mental and emotional, ruined his preparation to be a priest, and blotted his memory of Cuddesdon. ... Nevertheless Cuddesdon was important to him. For later he also believed that the motor accident and its consequences could have destroyed his morale, but for the tranquil worship of the little

Oxfordshire village which for the time was his base. ... The place was a port in the storm.'¹ Bishop Michael seldom spoke of these traumatic times, and what can be known now of these events is summed up sensitively and fairly by Chadwick, who was close to him, especially in the closing years. Yet it was to Cuddesdon that he first returned upon retirement in 1974, perhaps unwisely, but always full of hope and expectation.

Bishop Michael combined shyness and high intelligence, and this rendered him deep in compassion but sensitive and reticent in expression. His face reflected these qualities at all times, except when it was transfigured by mirth, for he shared with Joan, his wife, a devastating wit. If joy is the hallmark of a saint, joy often bubbled out of him as much by gesture as by word. There was also a purity, if wariness, about his approach to friendship; but once this was secured, his generosity of spirit was infectious. Yet at the same time he wore the air of someone familiar with rejection and misunderstanding. He appeared quickly pained as he heard some unhappy news or shared some intractable problem. His pastoral sense arose from a heart that had been broken on several occasions. He told little of his own experience of suffering, but he always communicated from out of it, as if from some hidden wellspring within him.

Yet to watch him at prayer, or celebrating the Eucharist, was to see a light of vision transfiguring the deep-set lines which had been etched by suffering, thought and sensitivity. The sense of God's presence and His glory was a constant theme of his preaching and teaching, and as his life drew towards its end, he used to insist that heaven was the goal of it all, and to its reality he seemed especially sensitive. He urged that Christians should become self-forgetful in the worship of God and in the service of other people. As a priest he embodied the meaning of sacrifice: costly offering in tender humility of the self to God in love of Him and in compassionate service of others. He once wrote to a young priest on the eve of ordination: 'I pray that your priesthood may be joyful because sacrificial, and sacrificial because joyful.'

The priesthood was central to his whole life and vision of Christianity and especially of being a bishop, and in this he was consciously guided by the example of Jesus, as remembered by the writer of the letter to the Hebrews: 'Ours is not a high priest unable to sympathize with our weaknesses, but one who has been tested in every way as we are, only without sinning.'[2] Towards the end of his life, he would return again and again to the great prayer of Jesus in St John 17, as if it contained the whole secret of the incarnation and of a Christian's relationship with God in Christ.

Serving within a church largely unmarked by martyrdom in its long history, Bishop Michael was plunged deeply from the beginning of his ministry into the abyss of darkness caused by suffering, and at times this seemed to set him apart from some around him. But the crucible of Cuddesdon equipped him in a unique way to deal with the spiritual demands of the twentieth century, in the Anglican Communion and well beyond it. For the twentieth century was a time of global suffering and upheaval, and of Christian martyrdom on a scale unprecedented since the third century.

The place of suffering was also the place of vision – a vision sustained by sacrificial prayer and sympathetic compassion, which can be traced throughout the books that he wrote. His first work, *The Gospel and the Catholic Church*, published in 1936, remains seminal. In its intensity and clarity of purpose it remains unique among his writings, for it enshrines, so far as writing ever can, the vision that was born within him during the years of his suffering and formation as a young priest. The phrase 'living through dying' encapsulates it, describing the indescribable experience of St Paul and all those who have followed him, the saints who have discovered that 'death is at work in us, but life in you'.[3]

Many years later, in 1966 as Archbishop of Canterbury, he wrote these words in a foreword to a little book called *Problems of Christian Belief*, which were talks he gave for the BBC:

> I have been through nearly all my life as a believing Christian. But that does not mean that I have found belief easy. Christian faith has been for me a constant process of wrestling, of losing and finding, of alternating night and day. For me the struggle is not between faith and unbelief so much as within faith itself. Faith is a sort of adventurous conflict in the midst of which certainty deepens. When the certainty passes, as it does for me, into a sense of peace and serenity it is none the less a costly peace, a peace in the heart of conflict.

The sensitivity of a Christian to human suffering prevents any facile statement, or acceptance, of the proposition that God is loving. Indeed belief that God is almighty and all-loving is strained for a sensitive Christian, until he or she passes on to see the divine way of dealing with suffering in the Cross of Christ. There the answer comes. But it is an answer not speculative but practical, for it is an answer valid only when the spirit of Christ crucified has been translated into human lives – lives which show what can be made of suffering in terms of heroic saintliness. Such lives are faith's most powerful witnesses, for just when the problem of evil oppresses us they assault us with the problem of good. The message that God is love will never be made convincing by facile statements, but only by Christians who share in that love in the spirit of Christ crucified.

✳ ✳ ✳

The seed of this conviction lies hidden in the first part of *The Gospel and the Catholic Church*. Its meaning then unfolds throughout his subsequent writings. Bishop Michael was convinced from his own experience that the gospel proclaimed by the life and suffering of the Church addressed the deepest needs of human beings. The existence of Christianity pointed beyond itself to the death of Jesus, and 'to the deeper issues of sin and judgement – sin in which Christians shared, judgement under which they stood together with the rest of mankind'.[4] A Christian is therefore someone who has faced, or been forced to face, often through suffering, the stark truth declared by St Paul that 'all alike have sinned'.[5] This experience is devastating in its impact, a 'veritable dying to self' and to the cocoon of delusions spun around it. The Church therefore 'points to the deeper problem of man himself' – hence its unpopularity in many quarters. Salt of the earth it may be, but salt is sharp and unpalatable, and a threat to what is corrupt; and that is sensed instinctively in the depths of the human heart.

'Christians are sent to be the place where the passion of Jesus is known and where witness is borne to the resurrection of the dead.'[6] The key word here is 'known' – how can this mystery be known? The sacraments of the Church, baptism and the

Eucharist, mediate this reality: on the altar, as St Augustine said, Christians see set before them that which they are called to become, and which by God's grace they are enabled to become. Just as Jesus 'knew whence he came and whither he was going', so too Christians discover at the foot of Calvary God's power, and the secret of Christ's way to the Father, 'whence they come and whither they go'. The language in the New Testament of participation in the dying and rising of Jesus is not just symbolic: it speaks of an actual experience that transforms human life.

The full meaning of the incarnation is revealed upon Calvary, where 'the Word was identified with mankind right down to the point of death, and enabled human beings to find unity through a veritable death to self'.[7] The force of this dying to self is captured in some words that remain from the moment when Bishop Michael was himself ordained priest. This was the most significant moment in his life, as he used later to say, 'I never fail to remember the day of the year when I was made a priest.' They are found in Chadwick's biography:

> Still my mind runs back to self. Cut it out: God is in me.
> He is my centre – let me only believe it, and His energy will
>   flood the whole of me, and self will be drowned.
> Let God be then alone in me – then in God we will find
>   ourselves – selfless, free, sons.
> Come God – my God is, and is in me, in you.
> Let God explode, burst from within, filling the whole of us –
>   away from self – just He.[8]

From his own experience he could assert that for the Christian and for the Church 'this dying is a stern reality'.

* * *

The root of all his spiritual theology lay in the Bible, and in a deep and sensitive reflection upon the meaning of its language. In a careful examination of crucial Old Testament passages, he unfolded the inner significance of the suffering servant tradition in Isaiah and the other prophets, and also in the psalms. He believed that 'the Old Testament has both its Church and its passion, and Christ is the fulfilment of both'.[9] This he was sure was the consistent witness of the New Testament in all its varied strands. Central to the later Old Testament tradition was the agony of innocent suffering, to which Job and the psalms pay eloquent testimony. 'The faith of Israel remains, while the passion of Israel is inescapable.'[10] This is echoed in the insistence of Jesus that the Son of Man had to suffer – in Greek *dei pathein* – in fulfilment of the scriptures: 'The Son of Man did not come to be served but to serve, and to give up his life as a ransom for many.'[11] This Bishop Michael believed constituted the common bedrock of the various gospel traditions.

The Church was born on Calvary: 'We must search for the fact of the Church not beyond Calvary and Easter but within them.'[12] As Jesus himself proclaimed: 'Unless a grain of wheat falls into the ground and dies, it remains that and nothing more; but if it dies, it bears a rich harvest.'[13]

> For through the lonely death, and the resurrection which seals its triumph, and the gift of the Spirit of him who died and rose, there is created a new Israel or Church of God, in which the gospel of God is proclaimed, brought to birth by a creative act of God. Thus the Church is Israel still, for by the Messiah's death it has been created and made a people unto God. The Church exists, because he died: his death is the centre of its existence, of its worship, and of the way of unity, which it offers to mankind.[14]

All that Bishop Michael taught about the nature of the Church and its unity is mirrored also in the experience of the individual Christian as the heart is broken before the Cross, drawn into the lonely agony of Jesus himself. The experience of Israel and of the Church are of one piece, and therein lies the clue to their final reconciliation, for 'in the isolation of Calvary Jesus alone is Israel, the son and the servant'.[15] Calvary is the place 'where the name, the glory, the will and the promises of God are seen'. Only as Jesus fulfils the destiny of Israel does he become the foundation of the Church: 'Jesus Christ, in his solitary obedience, *is* the Church.' He concludes: 'It is indeed a paradox that the death of Jesus, an event of utter isolation from men and God, should be the means of fellowship between men and God, and between men and one another.'[16] This insistence on the solitary nature of Christ's sufferings, and the agony of his being rejected and humiliated, points to another inescapable aspect of living through dying to which Christians are called, and with which Bishop Michael was familiar. Christian experience of this bitter suffering and of its awful loneliness opens the eyes of the heart to the world's tragedy:

> If Jesus is near to humanity in the joyful contact of his ministry in Galilee, teaching and healing and blessing, he is nearer still as he goes to the Cross. Christ enters by way of the Cross into nearer and nearer contact with the grim human realities of sin and creatureliness and death.[17]

This last phrase proved prophetic as the twentieth century unfolded with all its horrors. People sensed in Bishop Michael one whose heart and sympathy had been enlarged by his own engagement with evil and suffering, and who could share in their pain, wherever he met them in the world. He pointed to the unanimous testimony of the writer of the letter to Hebrews, and of St Paul, reflecting on the meaning of Christ's agony in the garden of Gethsemane:

> The New Testament writers know man, for all his achievements, as a dying creature, confronted with the boundary and the fear of death; and death sums up the truth about man when he is seen in the light of the eternal God. Now into this death the Son of God came, tasting both the fear of death, and the fact of death, and the moral meaning of death.[18]

This is the solemn significance of St Paul's words: 'Christ was innocent of sin, and yet for our sake God made him one with human sinfulness, so that in him we might be made one with the righteousness of God';[19] an insight amplified in the letter to Hebrews: 'In the course of his earthly life Jesus offered up prayers and petitions, with loud cries and tears, to God who was able to deliver him from death. Because of his devotion his prayer was heard: son though he was, he learned the full meaning of

obedience through his sufferings.'[20] The words of Newman's
great hymn, 'Praise to the Holiest in the height', always meant a
great deal to Bishop Michael, and his words make an ample commentary on their message:

> For our Lord enters so deeply into the meaning and the pain
> and the darkness of our race cut off from God by sin, that he
> seems momentarily to lose the vision of the Father; and he is
> never more man's brother and never more *totus in nostris* –
> one with us – than in the cry of dereliction. In Galilee he was
> near to men, but the full meaning of sin before God was not
> disclosed. On Calvary he is near to men in the death which
> sums up and reveals what man is, as creature and as sinner
> before God. Thus he came in order to die; so as to be man, in
> man, of man, going whither men must go. And his coming to
> die does not mean the negative act of a suicide seeking self-
> destruction, but the positive act of one whose love embraces
> man and all that is man's. 'Whither thou goest, I will go.'[21]

✳ ✳ ✳

Bishop Michael was deeply influenced by the teaching of Charles
Gore and other Anglican theologians of the early twentieth century in the emphasis they placed upon the meaning of the self-
emptying of Christ – sometimes described as 'kenotic theology' –
drawn from the language of St Paul's letter to the Philippians.[22]
The obedience of Jesus meant that 'his selfhood is so laid down,
that his power and authority centre in his humiliation'.[23] The
gospel story that most summed this up in his mind was that of
Jesus washing his disciples' feet in St John 13. Long meditation on
the meaning of this event, about which he often spoke publicly
and in private, left a profound mark on the way Bishop Michael
expounded St John's gospel. His approach was summed up long
ago by St Augustine, who observed that 'proud man could only be
saved by the humble God'. So Bishop Michael concluded that
'this self-abandonment does not belong to the earthly life alone,
for it is the experience in history of the self-giving of the eternal
God'.[24] He interpreted St Paul's poetry in Philippians 2 as pointing to the profoundly sacrificial nature of the incarnation:

For St Paul the incarnation is in itself an act of sacrifice than which none is greater: Christmas is as costly in self-giving as is Good Friday. Only the crucifixion is the deepest visible point of the divine self-giving, which entered history at Bethlehem and which begins in heaven itself.[25]

Responding to the insight of the book of Revelation which speaks of 'the Lamb slain since the foundation of the world',[26] and to the theology implicit in the letter to the Hebrews, he would often quote with approval the words of one of his earliest mentors, P.T. Forsyth: 'There was a Calvary above which was the mother of it all.' Returning to St John's gospel, he asserts that 'the Son finds in the Father the centre of his own existence; it implies a relationship of death to himself as himself. This attitude and action of the Son in history reveals the character of the eternal God, the mutual love of Father and Son.'[27] The disciples of Jesus are called to share in this self-giving love by his prayer recorded in chapter 17, 'to the end that men may make it their own and be made one'.

The radical conclusion is that 'the death to self as self, first in Christ and then in the disciples, is the ground and essence of the Church'.[28] These fragments, which he wrote on the eve of his own ordination as a priest, reveal the force with which Bishop Michael experienced this at a moment of profound self-offering to God:

> 'My grace is sufficient for thee.' How I do need to look away
>   from self to God; I can only find satisfaction in Him.
> My heart to love Him; my will to do His will;
> My mind to glorify Him; my tongue to speak to Him and of
>   Him;
> My eyes to see Him in all things;
> My hands to bring whatever they touch to Him;
> My all only to be a real 'all', because it is joined to Him.
> And this will be utter joy – no man can take it away.
> Self, self-consciousness, self-will, the self-centre cut away,
> So that the centre which holds all my parts is God.[29]

This self-surrender is losing in order to find, it is no self-destructive act. For Bishop Michael believed that in Christ 'God's power is manifested in self-emptying love, and to be made man, to die, to be buried is of the power of God no less than is the creation of the world. Thus in the nothingness of the death and the tomb there is a love so mighty that He lives and fills all things.'[30] God the Creator acts therefore as God the re-creator of human persons. Instead of the 'self' individually conceived, there is found the 'person' held within the eternal love, and defined in relationship to God and to others.

> He died to self, morally by the will to die throughout his life, actually by the Crucifixion. He died with men, as man, coming by the water and the blood. God raised him, and in the death and resurrection the fact of the Church is present. For as he is baptised into man's death, so men shall be baptised into his. As he loses his life to find it in the Father, so men may, by a veritable death, find a life whose centre is in Christ and in the brethren. 'One died for all, therefore all died.' To say this is to describe the Church of God.[31]

* * *

'Living through dying' is, however, as much about living as about dying. The resurrection of Christ becomes something that Christians experience within themselves. The Church exists to mediate this reality and to enable Christians to bear it. The key word in Bishop Michael's mind was fellowship – translating the Greek word *koinonia*, which has since become a term central to ecumenical language and experience. He defines it as something 'deeper than ecstasy and emotion'. 'It penetrates into the whole lives of the disciples, so that the word *koinonia* describes a oneness in thought, in mind, and in the sharing of goods, of sufferings, and of a life which is not their own but Another's.'[32] He observes that throughout the New Testament 'the fellowship and the death [of the Messiah] are inseparable'. Christians find themselves 'alive in one another and in the Spirit of the Lord Jesus'. So he concludes: 'Not only did the crucifixion make possible the giving of the Spirit, but the life bestowed by the Spirit is a life of which crucifixion is a quality, a life of living through dying.'[33]

This is the life-long meaning of baptism, which determines the unfolding character of a person's spiritual experience, and it is sustained by sharing in the mystery of the Eucharist. This is a 'real action of God who recreates: the best commentary is found in the saints, whose hidden life has been their response to the fact of their baptism'.[34] The description of the Church as the body of Christ is again not simply symbolical: but as a true symbol it participates in the divine reality to which it points – the living through dying of Christ himself, within which Christians find the meaning to their existence and experience.

Bishop Michael was quite adamant that a Christian can never escape from life within the Church: 'It is a part of his own existence since it is a part of Christ himself. Without the Church the Christian does not grow, since Christ is fulfilled in the totality of all his members.'[35] This led him to a rare note of outright condemnation: 'Individualism therefore has no place in Christianity, and Christianity verily means its extinction. The individual Christian exists only because the body exists already. In the body the self is found, and within the individual experience the body is present.'[36] To modern Christians comes therefore this sharp reminder of St Paul: 'You do not belong to yourselves; you were bought at a price.'[37] In this approach, Bishop Michael took on the centrifugal tendencies in the Church as well as in society at large. He swam against this tide throughout his life, standing for a deeper and more organic view of reality, and of the ultimate unity and spiritual meaning of all human relationships.

Bishop Michael was always confident and full of joyful hope about the possibilities for Christian life. Referring to the way in which the death and resurrection of Christ govern every aspect of Christianity, he asserts: 'History cannot exhaust the meaning of these events, since in them the powers of another world are at work, and the beginnings of a new creation are present. God is in Christ reconciling the world to himself: the powers of evil have been overcome, and a new order is entering the life of humanity and of nature.'[38] But he repudiated any form of triumphalism, wherever it occurred in the life of the Church:

The heavenly status of the Church can hardly be exaggerated, but it is a sovereignty of dying and risen life, it is apprehended through faith in the Cross, its power is known in humiliation, and neither the resurrection of Christ nor the place of the Church beside him can be perceived by the mind of the world.[39]

This is a crucial declaration, as it accounts for the strong connection Bishop Michael discerned between the heavenly dimension of the Church's existence and its capacity to enter deeply into the world's darkness. In his vision the glory of God is to be found at the place where the light of Christ penetrates the darkness of human sin and evil. Christians are called to follow that light wherever it may lead, and at whatever personal cost.

In this way the experience of suffering is transformed. Christians struggle with the effects of sinfulness within themselves, but they also wrestle with the problem of pain and tragedy in nature and in humanity:

> Here too they recognise the passion of Christ. They do not fear the struggle, for pain has been used by Christ, and has been given a new significance; and taught by him, Christians can use it for love, for sympathy and for intercession. It enables them to enter more deeply into his passion, it helps to wean them from any contentment with the present order and its false values, it makes them 'members one of another' in a unity springing from the Cross and pointing to a glory which is to be revealed.[40]

Bishop Michael supported this contention with words from Karl Barth's commentary on St Paul's letter to the Romans. Here as elsewhere at this stage in the development of his biblical theology, he was influenced by Barth's critique of any theology which effectively distanced God in His impact upon human life and suffering, and which failed to address the dire need of mankind in the years after the First World War.

* * *

The importance of the inner spiritual conflict at the heart of Christian life was reflected in the emphasis Bishop Michael placed on the need for frequent confession. As his life drew towards its close, he often lamented the decline of this practice within the Church of England. He never underrated the inroads of sin, nor was he content with any psychological approach that directly or indirectly sought to mitigate it. The costliness and humiliation experienced in confession was to his mind part of the bearing of the Cross; but it was also giving God opportunity to restore the damage within a human person. It opened a secret wellspring of spiritual renewal and strength, an inner martyrdom from which life-giving love could flow to others. He describes this stream of compassion in these moving words:

Like Christ, the Church is sent to execute a twofold work in the face of the sufferings of men; to seek to alleviate them, to heal them and to remove them, since they are hateful to God. Yet when they are overwhelming and there is no escape from them, to transfigure them and use them as the raw material of love. So in every age Christians have fought to remove sufferings, and have also borne witness to the truth that they can be transfigured and can become the place where the power of God is known. So in these two ways – the inner conflict with sin and the outer bearing of pain – the Church is a scene of continual dying; yet it is the place where the sovereignty of God is known and uttered, and where God is still reconciling the world to Himself. Here life is given in abundance, and here the faithful discern the peace of the resurrection.[41]

He concludes this opening part of *The Gospel and the Catholic Church*, in which he has set forth the core of his vision and experience, by talking about the 'not yet' in Christian faith. He himself lived as one familiar with this mysterious boundary between life now and eternal life, between experience and hope, between sorrow and joy. His words capture the vantage point from which he viewed the Church's life, and the progress of an individual Christian's pilgrimage towards God:

The puzzle of the 'not yet' speaks of the inexhaustible and unimaginable character of God's purpose: He has redeemed us, but it is not yet made manifest what we shall be. He has given Himself to us, but He has still more to give. And this 'not yet' throws further light on the meaning of the Church. It exists in faith and hope, in a hidden life in Christ, by a power, which can never be known in terms of the world's ideas of progress. It is the place where human personality is lost and yet found and enriched, and where all mankind shall be made one by the death and resurrection of Christ.[42]

2

The Servant's Sacrifice

O Lord, my Father and my God – thou art the giver of all good
gifts.
In all that thou givest – and always thou givest – thou givest
only the good.
Though it come through adversity, vexation, sorrow, make me
apprehend that good,
The wisdom of thy law, the height and depth of thy love;
Let me apprehend, accept, give thanks.
In all that thou givest, thou givest, not just the good, but the
best;
Nothing less wouldst thou give, nothing else canst thou give;
And that best is Thyself, nothing less, nothing else:
Thyself given once and wholly in thy Son,
Thyself given always and without measure in thy Spirit,
Thyself given visibly in thy sacrament, but invisibly everywhere,
Unfailingly, without limit, unalterably, world without end.

*

'Sacrificial because joyful, joyful because sacrificial': these words
encapsulate the ethos of Bishop Michael's spiritual theology. The
concept and reality of sacrifice lay at the heart of his approach to
God. He believed also that it left a transforming impression on
the language of the Bible. The insistence of Jesus that the Messiah
'had to suffer' indicated that this theme of purposeful suffering
runs like a golden thread throughout both the Old and the New
Testaments. Meanwhile, the human experience of suffering, in
its threatening as well as its self-sacrificing impact, is common to
all men and women. The genius of Christianity lies in its ability
to make a life-giving connection between that experience and the
long tradition of God's self-revelation enshrined in the Bible.
Human suffering seen in the light of Christ's own experience

points to the very heart of God as Creator, in whom self-giving love, expressed in sacrifice and responded to by sacrifice, is the very fountain of life itself. That is why Calvary reveals the deep truth of an eternal reality – 'the Lamb slain since the foundation of the world.'[1]

> The Church proclaims the wisdom of God, set forth in its very essence in the crucifixion of Jesus, a wisdom learnt when men and women are brought to the crisis of repentance and to the resulting knowledge of self and of God. The wisdom of the Cross seems at first to deny the wisdom of the Spirit of God in the created world; it scandalises men's sense of the good and the beautiful. But Christians who have first faced the scandal, discover in the Cross a key to the meaning of all creation. The Cross unlocks its secrets and its sorrows, and interprets them in terms of the power of God.[2]

The message of the Bible is that true sacrifice is essentially life giving. This is what Abraham discovered when he went up the mountain willing to sacrifice his only son, Isaac.[3] Influenced by contact with civilizations which practised human sacrifice, he was led to believe that this was the highest thing he could offer to God, even though it would appear to have been contrary perhaps to his normal practice of animal sacrifice as a nomad. The highest and the best for God was the principle he followed, whatever the personal cost to himself: a unique offering in response to a unique gift. In this intuition he was right, even if his experience marked an end to human sacrifice for him and his descendants. For in his willingness to offer up his only son he was as close to the heart of God as any human being could be: wrong at one level perhaps, but right at another, for 'God so loved the world that He gave His only Son'.[4] Thereafter all animal sacrifices within the worship of Israel would serve as symbols of this deeper principle of sacrifice, which would in the end be vindicated and given its fullest expression in the death of Jesus on the Cross.

> The essence of sacrifice is the giving of life, though death is the mark and the significant fact about that life, making it forever 'the life whereof the abiding characteristic is to have died.' ...

Christians look back to the sacrifice of Calvary, and they look up to the eternal sacrifice, which it reveals.[5]

* * *

Sacrifice is also the only path to holiness, which may be described as the sense of God, of being with God, and of becoming in the end like God: 'crucifixion – truth – the life of holiness, all these are linked.'[6] For Bishop Michael, this path was supremely indicated in the great prayer of Jesus in chapter 17 of St John's gospel. The heart of that prayer lies in these words of Jesus: 'Consecrate them by the truth; your word is truth. As you sent them into the world, I have sent them into the world, and for their sake I consecrate myself, so that they too may be consecrated by the truth.'[7] The meaning of these words constitutes also the message of the letter to the Hebrews, where Christ is portrayed as the true high priest, one who was 'made like his brothers in every way, so that he might be merciful and faithful as their high priest before God, to make expiation for the sins of the people. Because he himself has passed through the test of suffering, he is able to help those who are in the midst of their test.'[8] This 'test' is the crucible of temptation and suffering, the enduring of the fire of divine love as it remakes human nature, 'for our God is a devouring fire'.[9]

The language of prayer is the mirror of this experience of sacrifice and sanctification. Citing the teaching of St Augustine, Bishop Michael spoke eloquently of the psalms as the source of this particular language of prayer and experience: 'The psalter is the utterance of the life and pain of the whole Church, since it is the utterance of Christ to whom belong both the Old Testament and the New: "He prays for us, as our priest; he prays in us, as our head; he is prayed to by us, as our God. Let us recognize then our words in him, and his words in us." '[10]

As countless saints have found throughout the centuries, within Judaism and Christianity, the psalms express the prayer of the heart, racked as it often is by suffering and confusion in the presence of God, or overwhelmed by a sense of His absence. They enshrine both the human tragedy and the human longing for God: 'The faith of Israel remains, while the passion of Israel is inescapable.'[11] The glory of God in the face of Jesus Christ is divine light transfigured by suffering in confrontation with the darkness of evil. The fact that, according to St Mark, Jesus died with the words of Psalm 22 on his lips points the way: 'My God, my God, why have you forsaken me?' In words again from Hebrews: 'It is a terrifying thing to fall into the hands of the living God.'[12] Throughout the psalms and the prophets, God's suffering servant speaks of the cost of sacrifice and sanctification, 'and God speaks to proclaim that the servant's sacrifice enables men to have deliverance and peace'.[13]

The poetry of the Bible, seen now in the light of the death and resurrection of Jesus, enables this vision to shine like a living gleam of gold through all its strata. For example, the declaration of the prophet Zechariah, 'They will look on him whom they have pierced',[14] is echoed again at the close of the New Testament, in the book of Revelation;[15] and also when Christ, pierced upon the Cross,[16] becomes the source of eternal salvation for all who trust in him.[17] As the first letter of St Clement further demonstrates, belief in the significance of Jesus as God's suffering servant lies at the foundation of all Christian belief and prayer; and the words of Jesus in St John's gospel prove to be prophetic of true spiritual experience: 'If anyone is thirsty, let him come to me and drink. Whoever believes in me, as scripture says, "Streams of living water shall flow from within him." '[18] Life flows out through those united to Christ, but at profound cost to him and also to them: the language of scripture mediates this spiritual reality and experience.

* * *

In a remarkable lecture to the Anselm Society, which he founded as Archbishop at Canterbury,[19] Bishop Michael pursued more deeply the pattern of the transformation of Jewish sacrificial language in the New Testament. Jesus is portrayed as the true Passover lamb whose blood secures the new covenant. He is the sin offering, the true atonement. He is also seen as the scapegoat, which bears away the sins of God's people. Another image is of the sacrifice that begins the era of the kingdom of God. Implicit here perhaps is the ancient offering of the first fruits, embodied in the custom of dedicating the first-born male child to God:[20] God's only Son now becomes the first-born from the dead. Finally there is the title, 'the Lamb of God', which originated at the beginning of St John's gospel as a cryptic Messianic title, but which was subtly transformed into a symbol of God's suffering servant as portrayed in Isaiah 53. Only a profound understanding of Christ, and what he meant to the earliest Jewish Christians, could account for this 'juxtaposition of hitherto incompatible imagery' around one person, and one event – Calvary.

To combine the pure sin offering of atonement with the scapegoat driven out of the camp into the desert was truly remarkable; but its root lay in the figure of the suffering servant:

Jesus offers to the Father an offering of a life of purity and perfect obedience; and in the self-same act he is taking upon himself the burden of the sins of the world – the total calamity of human sin, grief, darkness, and estrangement. That is, in a way, the heart of the gospel of Jesus: the Jesus who glorifies the Father by a perfect obedience is the same Jesus who enters the darkness, the whole situation of human sin. ... The love whereby Jesus makes his pure and perfect offering is the same love whereby Jesus identifies himself completely in the bearing of the load of human calamity.[21]

Then there is the fusion of the victorious king and the self-sacrificing priest. In St John's gospel, Jesus dies as the true Passover lamb, but his crucifixion is an enthronement, a revelation of divine glory and purpose to which the entire gospel has been leading: 'The victory that is won by self-giving love; the self-giving love which is victorious.' Once again the picture of the Lamb upon the throne in the book of Revelation is highly significant: 'The throne denoting sovereignty, the Lamb denoting sacrifice.'

Finally there is the subtle interweaving of Old Testament language, notably in the letter to Hebrews, by which Jesus is portrayed as the true high priest, offering to God a unique sacrifice 'as man for man'. Hidden within this unique self-offering is a glimpse of the divine self-offering, now revealed as lying at the heart of the world's existence, because it is at the heart of God's own existence, as Father, Son and Holy Spirit:

> He is Son in terms of being priest, and priest in terms of being Son. This is a tremendously suggestive thought, and the possibilities of this are drawn out in one striking phrase: 'Christ offered himself without spot through the eternal Spirit.'[22] When Christ offered himself in time and history, it was in virtue of some eternal characteristic: perhaps in virtue of an eternal character, or through the power of the Spirit that is eternal.[23]

The challenge, he says, is to 'see the atonement in its own light – not fitting Jesus Christ into pre-existing concepts, but rather letting our view of the pre-existing concepts be twisted round by the fact of Jesus himself'.[24] One-sided caricatures of the atonement misrepresent its meaning, or in reaction rob it of its power to save by reducing it to exemplary symbolism.

> Christ comes as the true sacrifice. He embodies ideal sacrifice, as the joyful response of the creature to the Creator. In Christ man is seen recovering his true destiny of cleaving to the Father in holy fellowship, for that good end for which human nature was created. But we also see in Christ, God dealing with the tragedy of sin and suffering. In describing how Christ, by his death and rising again, dealt with the tragedy of human sin, none of the particular sacrificial images, of themselves, suffice. If we identify the doctrine of the atonement with any single one of them in isolation we get a totally inadequate presentation of Christ. The meaning of Christ's atonement is in that blending of sacrificial images, which he himself made.[25]

Christians are called to offer to God a living sacrifice, which in His hands will prove to be life giving to them, and through them to others as well. The influence of long meditation upon and celebration of the consecrating prayer in *The Book of Common Prayer* is always evident in the way Bishop Michael speaks of this spirit of sacrifice:

Almighty God, our heavenly Father, who of thy tender mercy didst give thine only Son, Jesus Christ, to suffer death upon the Cross for our redemption; who made there by his one oblation of himself once offered, a full, perfect, and sufficient sacrifice, oblation, and satisfaction for the sins of the whole world.

* * *

O Lord and heavenly Father, we thy humble servants entirely desire thy fatherly goodness mercifully to accept this our sacrifice of praise and thanksgiving; ... and here we offer and present unto thee, O Lord, ourselves, our souls and bodies, to be a reasonable, holy, and living sacrifice unto thee.[26]

The Christian 'sacrifice of praise and thanksgiving' is to be 'worship offered by mind and heart',[27] in fulfilment of the teaching of Jesus that 'true worshippers will worship the Father in spirit and in truth'.[28] This sacrificial worship is the path to holiness, and to life in all its fullness. For creation flows from sacrifice, and re-creation entails sacrifice also, by God in Christ, and by human beings in union with him. This pattern is already evident in the created order,[29] and in human life, notably within the family and among friends, where self-sacrificing love and forgiveness underpin all secure human relationships.

The Bible has the resurrection as its key. ... For the God who reveals Himself is also the God who created the world. Therefore the theme of the gospel, life-through-death, does not come as wholly strange to the world. Rather it is like a pattern already woven into nature and into the life of man. Though it is blurred by human sinfulness, this pattern is not obliterated; and throughout all life there runs, however faintly perceived, a law of living through dying, a law whose presence testifies that man is made in the image of God.[30]

The resurrection is therefore the beginning point for understanding how sacrifice can be life-giving, and how holiness can emerge through pain and suffering. The resurrection of Jesus revealed the true meaning of his life and death, and also the goal of human life in him; for in the words of the ancient creed *Quicunque vult* 'Christ took human nature into God'. Only by a personal union with Christ himself, by a willing sharing in his own death and risen life, can sin and death and all that damages human life be overcome. Those who wrote the New Testament saw the life of Christ in a double perspective, the inevitability of his suffering, but also the light of his resurrection: 'It corresponded to their own discovery that to share in the sufferings of Christ was to know his triumph: "always bearing about in the body the dying of Jesus, that the life of Jesus may be manifested in our body."'[31] This was the secret discovered later by the martyrs, that narrow and afflicted path, which is 'the road along which those who are Christ's may pass to a fuller sharing in his life'.[32]

> The Crucifixion is not a defeat needing the resurrection to reverse it, but a victory, which the resurrection quickly follows and seals. The 'glory' seen in the Cross is the eternal glory of the Father and the Son; for that eternal glory is the glory of self-giving love, and Calvary is its supreme revelation. So it is that the centre of apostolic Christianity is crucifixion-resurrection, for life-through-death is the principle of Jesus' whole life; it is also the inner essence of the life of Christians; and it is the unveiling of the glory of the eternal God. So utterly new and foreign to the expectations of men was this doctrine that it seems hard to doubt that only historical events could have created it.[33]

Suffering can never be evaded for long in this life, and it is a mistake to nurture too sentimental an understanding of the love of God. For in creation there is much that appears pitiless and apparently wasteful, and this is evident through all the long ages of earth's existence. God is not afraid to use suffering as an instrument of His creating purpose. In Christ, however, He has revealed the love behind His purpose, love which invites human beings to place themselves willingly into his hands, and to make their own Christ's prayer, 'Thy will be done'. This is the meaning of baptism, and of the life in Christ of which St Paul speaks in his letters:

The old world continues with its contradictions and its sufferings, but by the Cross and resurrection these very contradictions
and sufferings can be transformed into things fruitful and creative wherein, by faith in the Crucified, the power of God may be
found. There is no escaping from the facts of this world. Rather
does membership within the world-to-come enable Christians
to see the facts of this world with the light of the Cross and
resurrection upon them, and to know that their own tasks are
but the working out of a victory that Christ has already won.[34]

The testimony of St Paul in 2 Corinthians and Philippians, and
elsewhere, is decisive for understanding how living through
dying leads to an experience of resurrection life and of eternity
here and now:

> He is ever near to the Cross in his own conflict with sin; in his
> bearing of sorrow, pain and humiliation when they come to
> him; in his bearing of the pains of others; in his increasing
> knowledge of what Calvary meant and means. But in all this
> he is discovering that the risen life of Jesus belongs to him, and
> with it great rejoicing.[35]

Perhaps the most potent image in the New Testament to account
for this process is that of 'birth-pangs'. It runs through many
strands of the apostolic witness, and later informed the testi-
monies of the early martyrs, notably for example St Ignatius of
Antioch. In St John's gospel Jesus predicts that his disciples will
experience something like this when he is crucified and raised;[36]
in St Luke he associates it with baptism, speaking of the con-
straint he feels he is under until all is accomplished.[37] St Paul
speaks in similar language about the driving force of the 'love of
Christ' in 2 Corinthians;[38] and in Galatians he addresses his
spiritual children as those for whom he is 'in labour all over
again until you come to have the form of Christ'.[39] Finally in
Revelation, the woman in labour threatened by evil is a symbol
of the Church enduring martyrdom in fulfilment of God's will.[40]
Travail in re-creation mirrors the travail which is evident in the
processes of the created world, as the divine purpose is being
fulfilled: in the words of St Paul: 'The whole created universe in

all its parts groans as if in the pangs of child-birth',[41] in anticipation of the emergence of the children of God.

But this is a moral and loving process, not inexorable as in nature. In human nature it rests upon consent and endurance. This is why Bishop Michael laid such stress upon the meaning of sanctification at the heart of the prayer of Jesus in St John 17: 'Consecrate them by the truth: your word is truth.'[42]

> The connection between sanctification and truth is of the utmost consequence. The disciples in their mission to the world are required to be 'not of the world' in two ways. They are to be consecrated to God in opposition to the world's self-pleasing: they are to represent the truth of God in opposition to the world's errors. The two requirements are inseparable, even as grace and truth are inseparable in the mission of Christ. ... There is no holiness apart from the theology which he reveals, and there is no imparting of the theology except by consecrated lives.[43]

✳ ✳ ✳

Herein lies the true significance of the *kenosis,* or the self-emptying of Christ of which St Paul speaks in Philippians 2. To this path all Christians are called, and indeed are initiated by their baptism. This path is trodden by continual *metanoia* or repentance, meaning a change and renewal of heart and mind: it is the only path towards the glory of God:

> The 'glory' is the utter self-giving of Christ to the Father, which, released by his death, and brought into touch with human lives by his Spirit, can become the new principle of self-giving within them, and can banish the old principle of self-centred selfishness. ... The glory of Christ's self-giving breaks the power of human sinful glory and self-esteem.[44]

This is the supreme message of St John's gospel; and for the Christian contemplating the picture it paints, 'the conscience is pierced by God's love and judgement'. These words, influenced by the thought of St Gregory of Nyssa, explain why:

There was the humiliation whereby Christ's mission was completed only in suffering and death. But if this humiliation was, viewed from one angle, a concealment of the divine glory, it was, viewed from another angle, only an aspect of that glory. That the Son of God could thus make his own the frustrations of human life and death was a signal manifestation of the glory of the divine self-giving. The mission of the Lord was at once the descent of one who trod the road of frustration, ignorance, pain and death, and the ascent of one who was realising in humiliation a glory, which had been his from all eternity.[45]

The roots of Bishop Michael's approach to the meaning of the atonement can be clearly seen in his major study of Anglican theology during the first half of the twentieth century, *From Gore to Temple*, published in 1960. His thinking followed that of Charles Gore, who regarded the incarnation as the foundation for the atonement – 'the paradox whereby one who is divine and the Creator humbled Himself to take upon Himself the creaturely life of man. It was for the deliverance of mankind that God so humbled Himself.'[46] He took to heart also the teaching of the Congregational divine, P.T. Forsyth, quoting his observation that 'Christ could be tempted because he loved; he could not sin because he loved so deeply'.[47]

It is in chapter four, 'The Doctrine of the Cross', that Bishop Michael shows his mastery of the classical Anglican tradition, taking his cue from the prophetic teaching of Henry Scott-Holland, revealing how 'Christ's sacrifice is no far-away fact to be shown and gazed upon. It draws us into itself.'[48] In the eyes of God, 'Christ, the forgiveness, becomes the one forgiven man'.[49] Thus to be 'in Christ' is to be changed in oneself, and liberated into a new relationship with God. The depth of this truth was demonstrated by the pastoral insight of R.C. Moberly, who envisaged this change as being profoundly penitential in character: to be 'in Christ' is to discover 'not only the grace of Christ who pardons us, but also the grace of Christ who is at our side in our contrition and confession – making it with us, and for us'.[50] This is the key to the meaning and significance of compunction in the spiritual life.

For Charles Gore, the gravity of sin meant that this atonement was wrought at supreme cost to God: 'God does forgive us, but it costs Him much.'[51] For all three theologians, 'the Eucharist was a constant interpreter of doctrine', echoing the poetry of Wesley and later of Bright, whose eucharistic hymns remain important and profound expressions of classical Anglican belief. The meaning of the Eucharist was also a fundamental theme in Gore's later work, *The Body of Christ*, which vindicated the teaching of St Augustine that 'this is the nature of Christian sacrifice, that the many become one body in Christ'.[52] In this way, concluded Bishop Michael, 'Calvary is kept at the heart of our approach to God', again remembering the words of St Augustine, 'proud man could only be saved by the humble God'.

The most recent star in this firmament of Anglican divines was William Temple, whom Bishop Michael revered with a personal devotion. The question of the suffering of God became acute after the ravages of the First World War, and it cast its shadow over the whole of twentieth-century theology, darkening as the full horrors of Nazism and Communism became apparent. Here Temple gave a judicious lead. In his book, *Christus Veritas*, he insisted that Christ is the key to understanding the inner nature of God Himself: the Cross reveals 'the cost whereby God wins the victory over the evil which He has permitted. All that we can suffer is within the divine experience.'[53] Temple concluded that it is truer to say that 'there is suffering *in* God than that God suffers'. This is because God is Love, and to love truly is often to suffer deeply; only in this way is life born and re-born. The important thing is that God suffers, not as one who is frustrated in the end, but as one who in this way is victorious in His unshakeable purpose.

* * *

The spiritual teaching of Friedrich von Hügel, whose influence upon Bishop Michael's spiritual theology was considerable, further deepened this insight. For Bishop Michael believed that so profound a belief about God's purpose rested not just upon doctrine rooted in the Bible, but also, as von Hügel indicated, on Christian lives consecrated to God in prayer and self-sacrifice within the life of the Church. The attention that Bishop Michael paid in this respect to two notable spiritual figures in nineteenth-century Anglican life is most revealing: F.D. Maurice, and R.M. Benson.

F.D. Maurice was born in 1805 and died in 1872; like Bishop Michael he was born a nonconformist and became an Anglican in 1830 after a radical youth. As chaplain to Guy's Hospital in London, he lectured in moral philosophy, publishing his most influential book, *The Kingdom of Christ*, in 1838. Despite some controversy, he was elected as professor of English literature at King's College, London in 1840, and became in due course professor of theology there in 1846. He was active in developing a Christian response to the contemporary pressures for social change, founding a workingmen's college in 1854. He became professor of moral philosophy at Cambridge in 1866, and was the author of several works relating the gospel to the modern world. Bishop Michael devoted an important study to him, publishing in 1951 a book called *F.D. Maurice and the Conflicts of Modern Theology*. This deals with many aspects of Maurice's influence and legacy, but at its heart lies a discussion of the atonement in his belief and thought.[54]

The axiom of Maurice's theology was his deep conviction that 'Christ is in every man'. By this he meant that 'God made man in His own image, the image which is perfectly known in Christ';[55] the life offered through the Cross and resurrection 'is none the less the life of our true and original selves' as human beings. As Jesus said, 'I have come that they may have life, life in all its fullness.'[56] This brought Maurice much criticism at the time, as it seemed to deny the reality of the Fall. But as Bishop Michael ably pointed out, in the fourth chapter of his book, this belief committed one to a far deeper sense of God's engagement with humanity in overcoming sin and evil. The Cross reveals the agony of God as in love he reaches out to seek and to save the lost. The differing response of those dying alongside Jesus on Calvary reveals the power of divine love, and its agony in weakness, unable to force repentance, but able to save to the uttermost those who turn to God. The Cross therefore reveals both the horror of hell, and the divine light descending into the darkness to bring hope beyond hope, by bearing the whole searing rejection caused by wayward human wills being manipulated by evil. These are Maurice's own words about the Cross:

> Since nowhere is the contrast between infinite love and infinite evil brought before us as it is there, we have the fullest right to affirm that the Cross exhibits the wrath of God against sin, and the endurance of that wrath by the well-beloved Son. For wrath against that which is unlovely is not the counteracting force to love, but the attribute of it. Without it love would be but a name, not a reality. And the endurance of that wrath or punishment by Christ came from his acknowledging that it proceeded from Love, and his willingness that it should not be quenched until it had effected its full loving purpose. The endurance of that wrath was the proof that he bore in the truest and strictest sense the sins of the world, feeling them with that anguish with which only a perfectly pure and holy being, who is also a perfectly sympathising and gracious being, can feel the sins of others. Whatever diminished his purity must have diminished his sympathy also. Complete suffering with sin and for sin is only possible in one who is completely free from it.[57]

Bishop Michael goes on to demonstrate how, faithful to the deepest and oldest traditions of the Church, Maurice presented a coherent theology of the atonement based entirely on an understanding of the nature of God's love, overturning cruder theories of penal substitution, and challenging shallow approaches which regarded the death of Jesus as salutary because exemplary. 'Christ satisfied the Father by presenting "his own holiness and love, so that in his sacrifice and death all his holiness and love came forth completely." '[58]

The roots of this insight lay deep in the Old Testament, as Maurice demonstrated: in Abraham offering up himself as he prepared to sacrifice his only son; in the humiliation of David, expressed in Psalm 51, 'which showed him that he had nothing of his own to offer; that he must come empty-handed, broken-hearted, to receive of God that which He alone could give – a right and true spirit'.[59] Maurice believed that 'there is a ground of sacrifice within the divine nature' which Jesus revealed by his relationship with his Father.[60] The Cross is truly the focal point for the whole gospel story of Jesus in his relationship with God and men. This is Maurice's very important conclusion, as cited in Bishop Michael's summing up:

> Sacrifice is not contingent upon sin; it is 'implied in the very original of the universe': 'it was expressed in the divine obedience of the Son before the worlds were', and 'the manifestation of it in the latter days was to take away sin, because sin and sacrifice are the eternal opposites.'[61]

Salvation therefore means 'union with Christ in the power of the Spirit, the replacing of the rule of sin by the rule of sacrifice'[62] within human nature; and the hard learning of that is the meaning of Christian life with all its hopes, frustrations and suffering. In his book, *Christus Consummator*, Maurice showed how 'sacrifice is the character of God, and the true principle of man, made in God's image'.[63] He believed that Christ revealed that underlying all sin and evil, this divine principle was unshakeable, being the key to the relationship between the Father and the Son, and to the giving of the Spirit. Christ as man also revealed that it is the principle underlying all truly human life, that sin seeks ever to destroy this vision, and that evil is often the distortion of this very principle of life. This can be seen in the ease with which sacrificial language is often applied to warfare, or to economic injustice, or to abuse within human relationships, with most damaging consequences.

Bishop Michael concluded that the lasting significance of Maurice's theology, most fully expressed in his book, *The Doctrine of Sacrifice*, was this: 'It brought back the unity of atonement and creation; it linked together the idea of sacrifice and the doctrine of the Trinity; it gave to many their first glimpse of the classic conception of the Cross as the divine victory.'[64]

In a way, Maurice was like the restorer of an ancient painting or icon, stripping back with a sure intuition the layers of defective insight, many of them derived from the polemics of the Reformation, which were reacting against distorted elements within the piety of the later Middle Ages in the West; and revealing afresh glimpses of the pristine vision known to the earliest generations of the Church. But Maurice was adamant also that this conversion of vision needed divine grace, because human ignorance was profoundly moral and spiritual in nature. Bishop Michael saw Maurice as 'at once a penitent and a Christian humanist',[65] who lamented the fall of human beings, but who also asserted their dignity and destiny, called to become children of God in union with Christ. Human spiritual and moral ignorance is only overcome by a costly *metanoia* or repentance: 'We know God only by a conversion of the whole man.'

* * *

R.M. Benson was a very different figure to F.D. Maurice. He was born in 1824 and died in 1915, having founded the Society of St John the Evangelist in Oxford, later known as the Cowley Fathers. He was educated at Christ Church, Oxford, and served as vicar of Cowley, where he was deeply influenced by John Keble, from whom he drew his inspiration to found a religious community of priests in 1865. This had the active support of Bishop Samuel Wilberforce of Oxford, and became a seminal influence in the revival of contemplative monastic life and mission within the Church of England, at home and abroad. Father Benson led a strictly ascetic life, and was a preacher and spiritual teacher of remarkable depth and demand.

Bishop Michael contributed a penetrating essay to a commemorative volume, published in 1980: his title was 'Bruising the Serpent's Head: Father Benson and the Atonement'. In it he indicated how Benson always united the Cross and the resurrection. These words of Benson seemed to him to be of crucial significance:

Christ triumphed on the Cross that we might go through death to victory, not that we might pass to victory without enduring death. Our victory can only be the victory of the dead. Only in proportion as we are dead with Christ can we share his victory. We little know how our eagerness for success thwarts the manifestation of the resurrection power by which alone the truly mortified life is to be perfected.[66]

Benson wrestled throughout his life with the demands of the gospel in the face of a society ruled increasingly by material wealth and imperial success. The religious communities that he founded or nurtured were a silent protest against some aspects of late Victorian England, as well as a determined attempt to regain the spiritual rigour of earlier centuries of the Church's life. Benson practised what he preached, and led a life of spiritual discipline which exerted a profound influence on many Christians in his own lifetime and after. Bishop Michael writes as one familiar with the spiritual struggle which Benson constantly described, and which he regarded as inescapable in genuine Christian discipleship.

Like Maurice, Benson believed that sacrifice expressed the true relationship between human beings and God, between creature and Creator: 'The sacrifice of their whole being to Him from whom it came.' In that sacrifice is found the source of true joy. The work of Christ revealed an act of new creation, filled with divine righteousness. In Bishop Michael's summing up, Christ risen from the dead 'is now the perfect sacrifice, the gift from God to man, and the gift from man to God'. Sharing in the Eucharist means sharing in this new life, with all its demands. But at the same time, it is a continuing dying to the world and its false values.

Baptism plunges a person into the mystery of God's atoning love, revealed but also hidden within the mystery of Christ. For Benson, 'not only the death but also the burial is a continuing process for the Christian believer throughout the whole of life'. This is the meaning of the ascetic life, the struggle with sin and evil which is at the same time the birth-pangs of a new creation, as a person is remade in the image and likeness of God revealed in Christ. As St Bernard once said: 'Life is given that we may learn how to love; time is given that we may find God.'

Benson also reckoned with the reality of conflict with evil, often reflecting on the mysterious promise in Genesis that the descendants of Adam and Eve would one day 'bruise the serpent's head'.[67] The Cross represents the divine victory over evil, once and for all. The liberation of human beings was won at supreme cost to Christ, and Christians are called to enter into that struggle and that cost, in order that the life-giving power of God's love can transform their lives and those of others. In Christ all the hatred of evil for human beings, made in God's image and likeness, comes to a head, and its deadly force is absorbed in the lonely suffering of Calvary. For Benson, the psalms were a window into the spiritual experience of Christ himself, and he called his commentary upon them *The War Songs of the Prince of Peace*.

In Benson's experience and preaching, conflict and victory were inextricably entwined while a Christian lived and prayed in this life. Taking up the Cross daily lay at the heart of true discipleship, and this was the only way of making sense of the suffering, opposition and frustration which is too often a Christian's lot. Bishop Michael drew attention to Benson's reflections upon the meaning of Christ's final discourse in St John 16 from his work, *The Final Passover*. He summed up Benson's teaching in these words: 'The world as the organism of sinful humanity hostile to God has been deprived of its power, and by dying to it we can live in freedom from it; but the world still remains as a snare until the Lord will return and his kingdom will be all in all.'[68]

To share in the suffering of Christ is a life-giving and transforming experience. The fruit of that experience gradually emerges as an enlarged sympathy and compassion, the discovery of Christ with us and within us, and through us reconciling all things unto himself.

3

One with Us

Inspire me, O Lord God, after the example of Christ to love my
neighbour,
Not as myself, but more than myself;
And where outward help is out of human reach
To have a true, lively, inward sympathy,
A pity and continuous prayer for the needs and agonies of
mankind.
Let those less than neighbours become more than brothers;
Let me love by prayer, help me pray them into strength,
Into thy mercies, into newness of life;
Let all be guests within my heart and loved in Thee,
Who loveth all, who loveth each, who art Love.

*

'There are people who make God near. This is the most marvel-
lous thing that one human being can do to another.' These words
of Bishop Michael's, remembered from a retreat and cited in
Chadwick's biography, were certainly true of him.[1] It was his
unique charism to be able to communicate by silence as well as
by word the reality and the love of God the Father – 'God the
Giver good' – a phrase he often repeated in his sermons. A brief
letter or even a telephone conversation could convey this just as
well as a more prolonged meeting or discussion. To embody the
truth of the gospel in this way, and to kindle love and confidence
in others is truly the hallmark of a saint.

From long meditation and at times painful insight, he mirrored
by a humble intuition the depths of God's love, and the cost of
that love. He pointed throughout his life and teaching to the
sureness of the divine purpose in the midst of suffering and darkness, regarding that suffering as a sign of the nearness of God's

involvement with human life. Chadwick quotes a comment by
Bishop Michael towards the very end of his life:

> Except for an agnostic patch in my teens, I've never doubted
> the existence of God. But I've sometimes found my faith in him
> so painful that I would rather have been without it. But that is
> the Christian way. Since the early tragedies of my life (the
> deaths of my mother and my brother) I have been as sensitive
> as anyone can be to suffering – to God himself taking on the
> darkness of alienation. That has made me very wary of any
> attempt to reconstruct the Christian faith without maintaining
> the place of the Cross of Christ in the redemption of suffering.[2]

This is a rare and important piece of personal testimony, and it
provides a key to his serenity in the midst of disappointment and
pain; for he regarded any share in the divine anguish as a mark of
friendship with God, the concomitant of love. From this conviction there flowed a sense of the unshakeable reality of God's
compassion, which he expressed through a sincere kindness and
interest towards each person who came to him as a priest and
friend. In this he was guided by the belief that Christianity is
about 'God finding us rather than we finding God', and that the
message of the Bible was 'to keep near to God, for in nearness to
Him things become different'. As a true Christian pastor he was
able to draw others into the saving presence of God Himself.

This emphasis on the love of God runs like a golden thread
throughout his writings. In one of his later works, *Jesus and the
Living Past*, Bishop Michael quotes with approval some words
of Friedrich von Hügel: 'We reach at last an apex of spirituality
which is at bottom the deepest self-giving of God in Jesus Christ
in the manger and the Cross.'[3] Bishop Michael himself gives this
summary of the nature of the Christian experience of God's love,
expressed in the pages of the New Testament:

> Here indeed is a picture of what the Christians were experi-
> encing; a new access to God, forgiveness, inner peace, joy even
> in the face of suffering, the facing of a stormy world with hope.
> How has this come about? It has come about by the shedding
> of God's love in their hearts when the Spirit was given to them.

But what does the love of God mean? It means the love shown in the death of Jesus for the ungodly. It is by that historical reference that the experience is defined and understood. The history did not only initiate the experience, it perpetually defines its character and inspires its renewal.[4]

Addressing the Benedictine monastic community at West Malling in Kent at the dedication of a new chapel, Bishop Michael said: 'The door of prayer towards heaven, towards the heart of God, is always a door of love into the world of human needs.'[5] This is the justification in part of the monastic vocation within the life of the Church: such places remind all Christians of the centrality of prayer. But awareness of God and his love leads also to awareness of human sin, personal and corporate. Bishop Michael was alert to both, and to the fatal connection between them, which the tragedies of the twentieth century demonstrated. He dealt eloquently with these truths in his classic book for those engaged in Christian ministry, *The Christian Priest Today*. There he insisted: 'Let the enhanced awareness of the sin of society lead the individual to see not less but more clearly in Christ's light that his sin is his own.'[6]

Whenever he heard of some blunder in the life of the Church, or some failing in a person, his face would be seized by a profound sorrow. He regarded sin as a lack of unselfish compassion, the sign of some inner failure of the vision of God and of His goodness. Blindness and insensitivity were particularly abhorrent to him temperamentally as well as by conviction. He sensed that sin is a terrible blight on human life, a fatal craving and tendency, which leads to the distortion of energy and often to the destruction of relationships. The medieval hymn to the Holy Spirit, which prays 'enable with perpetual light the dullness of our blinded sight', is close to his own perception and teaching. In a charge to those he was ordaining he issues this call to repentance – the changing of heart and mind, which lies at the root of the gospel:

This turning and change of mind are God's gift, and they are a turning and a change of mind towards God. We begin with a glimpse of the vision of God in His power and wonder and beauty and goodness. We praise Him for His greatness as Creator, for His mercy as redeemer and for His continuing loving kindness to ourselves. And a central point within this vision is the Cross of Calvary where Christ died for us. In this turning towards Him and the change of our mind towards Him there come the realization of our littleness and insignificance as His creatures, the absurdity of our pride and selfishness and fear, the shame of our ingratitude. We see our-selves in His light, exposing every corner of our being to Him. We grieve bitterly, and we rejoice in the truth. But we are sinners, and we cannot climb up again by our own act. Impotent, undeserving, we await His act, the words '*absolvo te*' – I forgive you.[7]

                              ✳ ✳ ✳

Steeped as he was within a spiritual tradition reaching back to the Tractarians and beyond, Bishop Michael's liberal political instincts, and the moral outrages with which his generation were confronted, made him no less trenchant and prophetic in his approach to the corporate sins of humanity. He believed firmly in the reality of divine judgement, and his thinking is most clearly stated in *The Christian Priest Today*. In a perceptive chapter[8] dealing with the problems of communicating the sense of God in modern society, he is adamant that a proper understanding of God's presence in judgement strips away false images of Him, and brings both Christian and critic face to face with the appalling suffering in the world:

> When men and nations turn away from God's laws, and prefer courses dictated by pride and selfishness to the courses dictated by conscience, calamitous results follow. God is not absent from the contemporary scene; He is present, present in judge-ment through the catastrophes, which follow human wilful-ness.[9]

He said this not from a position of episcopal superiority but because he believed simply that the law of God could no more be denied than the law of gravity: if gravity governs physical existence on earth, self-giving love is the invisible principle that governs relations between humans and with God Himself. The abuse of nature, and the abuse of human nature are two sides of the same self-destructive tendency. In the years since his death, the deepening ecological crisis, and the perpetual frustration of poverty and economic injustice in international relationships have given added force and urgency to his message.

But this uncomfortable message is to the Church as well as to society: 'The Church shows the message of divine judgement to the world as she sees the judgement upon herself and begins to mend her ways.'[10] Once again only a Christ-centred approach can interpret the meaning of divine judgement, and governing this is the profound vision of St John's gospel: 'This is the judgement: that light has come into the world, but people preferred darkness to light because their deeds were evil.'[11]

> It must be in the figure of Jesus crucified and risen that we present the divine judgement and mercy. I see no other way of bringing the themes of sovereignty, power, compassion, and judgement home to our contemporaries, except in terms of Jesus in whom these divine actions are focused.[12]

✳ ✳ ✳

To be a Christian is to be brought face to face with Christ, and with the world's need as a result of human sin. Repentance and reform have to begin within the heart and mind of the individual person. In *The Christian Priest Today*, and elsewhere, for example in *Be Still and Know*,[13] Bishop Michael lamented the decline of the practice of private confession within the Church of England. His verdict was that 'the failure to confess is in line with the failure to pray',[14] and he stated his understanding of the nature and importance of confession within the Anglican tradition at some length.[15]

He was confident about the place of confession within the tradition of *The Book of Common Prayer*, but he insisted upon its essentially voluntary character. He carefully set forth the classical arguments for its use: the desire to be thorough before God in penitence, and the willingness to endure some sense of pain and cost in so doing. Important too in his mind was the fact that God's word of forgiveness in Christ comes through the Church's witness and ministry; and the belief that the word of absolution is an evangelical and sacramental act, which draws someone close to the person and ministry of Jesus himself in the gospels, into 'a meeting with Jesus as wonderful and decisive as meeting him in Holy Communion'.[16]

He spoke from long practice when he described the role of an Anglican priest seeking to hint and suggest ways of spiritual development, and turning his or her face against a more dominating role. He was sure from his own regular experience as a penitent that making one's confession 'can bring a Christian vividly near to Christ crucified'.[17] He recognized that there were often two typical reasons for confession: either trauma or conversion resulting in a sense of desperate spiritual need, or the more routine if no less demanding path of those seeking to follow God's call to the path of holiness, and who accept its humiliation as part of the bearing of the Cross of Christ.

His view of what needed to be confessed was all-embracing: not just individual lapses and weaknesses, but 'our whole condition of failure' to be exposed to the cleansing of the divine light. 'The light of absolution will then penetrate the entire self',[18] and by this process a person can grow into a truer relationship with God Himself. For priests in particular he believed that this was an indispensable discipline, and a sure road to sustained spiritual renewal:

> It is when going to confession requires a sheer discipline of the will that a new and creative aspect of it may begin to emerge; the act of will in confessing may enable you to escape vagueness and drift and to regain a true picture of yourself. Then you may find in new ways how the loving-kindness of God can hide, as it were, beneath the recesses of your failure, and you are humbled by discovering how God can use you in spite of yourself.[19]

He conducted confessions with a discreet, self-effacing but business-like air, and he was always most strict about the confidential 'seal' of the confessional, even to the extent of refusing to confirm that he had been in church hearing confessions.

His deep attentiveness focused the attention upon what was essential, and his own advice afterwards was brief and almost delicately posed. He invariably directed the penitent to some collect, psalm or piece from the gospels to serve as a penance, and his general approach was to instil encouragement in the face of repeated failure and disappointment. The impression etched in the memory and the heart was that by confession a person found themselves at the feet of Christ and at the heart of the Church's mysterious life.

He used to emphasize that generosity and gratitude to God after confession serve as a sure antidote to human pride, frustrations and delusions; this spirit corrects many wrong attitudes and therefore heals human relationships as well. Humility is the goal of confession, because God Himself is humble. Bishop Michael's goal was to bring people close to God as Father, and to train them in the painful and life-long business of self-examination in His presence. In this way, he believed, the priest serves as a true intermediary in the soul-searching process whereby Christians place themselves willingly into the hands of the living God.

* * *

The writer of the letter to the Hebrews declares, however, that 'it can be a terrifying thing to fall into the hands of the living God',[20] and that 'our God is a devouring fire'.[21] Elsewhere he asserts: 'The Word of God is alive and active. It cuts more keenly than any two-edged sword, piercing so deeply that it divides soul and spirit, joints and marrow; it discriminates among the purposes and thoughts of the heart. Nothing in creation can hide from Him; everything lies bare and exposed to the eyes of Him to whom we must render account.'[22] The letter to Hebrews guided the way in which Bishop Michael approached the whole spiritual purpose of the priesthood in this area of pastoral ministry, as he glimpsed the deeper life-giving purpose of God Himself in the painful re-creation of human persons. It informed also his penetrating critique in *The Christian Priest Today* of the reasons often adduced for the decline of confession in the face of modern society and its values.[23]

The classical word for this spiritual process of divine healing is compunction – the painful but joyful unlocking of the human heart by the scalpel of God's love: it is for this that we pray in the words – 'Come Holy Spirit, fill now the hearts of your faithful people, and kindle within us the fire of your love.' Perhaps the best way of approaching the meaning of compunction and its effect is to consider the story of the paralysed man in the gospel. According to the earliest account in St Mark,[24] this miracle revealed Jesus as the Messiah empowered by God to forgive human sins; it also marked the beginning of opposition to him by the religious authorities. It is a story that juxtaposes sharply personal and corporate sin. This man lived in a very religious society that regarded cripples as punished by God, perhaps an inevitable reaction in a place where there was no reliable medical care. Religious teachers, who regarded such people as ritually unclean, reinforced this instinct. The chronically sick became scapegoats for a society fraught by fear, pain and insecurity.

Jesus performed a double miracle by curing the man's paralysis and declaring that this signified the complete forgiveness of this person's sins and sense of guilt, his inner and hidden paralysis, restoring him to social life as well. The man's psychological state can only be guessed at: perhaps he had caused his own suffering, or perhaps he was trapped by an imposed sense of guilt and alienation from God and society. The action of Jesus thus challenged a whole web of values, fears and attitudes.

Early Christians frequently associated this story with baptism, regarding the man's friends as representing the sponsors who brought a person to the Church to experience salvation through Christ. These friends showed great faith, effort, determination and courage. The paralysed man represented fallen Adam, who, in the words of St Augustine, 'had no power of himself to help himself'. He represents how human beings actually appear in the sight and presence of God; and this is true of each of the healing miracles of Jesus.

The unlocking of this paralysis may be the work of one traumatic moment, as in the case, it appears, of St Paul on the road to Damascus, or more often of a lifetime's fitful penitence and pain; but the process is a participation in the joy of resurrection, as the language of the gospel text makes clear. It is the restoration of a human person in the image and likeness of God himself, to the destiny for which human beings were first created. The action of God's healing compassion is not confined however to the individual person; but through that person's redemption, human society and its values are being challenged and transformed also. Instrumental within this laborious process are other people, drawn to collaborate with God in his work of healing love.

* * *

Christians are called therefore to enter into God's saving work through their own compassion and sympathy. How they care for others and how they pray for them is the test of how Christ-like their love is becoming. Intercession lies at the heart of Christianity, for an act of kindness must also be an act of prayer, and prayer must serve where practical acts cannot be achieved. As in these words of St Gregory the Great: 'Your prayers are at work where you are not; your holy works are evident where you are.'[25]

Addressing the Benedictine community at West Malling, Bishop Michael indicated how the life of a religious community serves as a focal point for the whole praying ministry of the Church, built upon the teaching of St Benedict – *laborare est orare, orare est laborare* – to work is to pray, and to pray is to work:

> Here prayer is the work, and this service of the world is itself the prayer offered to the most High God, on the world's behalf. And this means an apartness like that of our Lord in the Judean desert: praying and fighting on behalf of us all, on behalf of the human race. It is apartness, a being with God, but always on behalf of the human race with its sins, its joys, and its sorrows.[26]

He regarded contemplation and intercession as two sides of the same coin, and in this his teaching was very close to that of his friend and supporter, Mother Mary Clare, who presided over the community of the Sisters of the Love of God, at Fairacres in Oxford, during his primacy at Canterbury. She once wrote that 'the person who prays stands at that point of intersection where the love of God and the tensions and sufferings we inflict on each other meet and are held to the healing power of God'.[27] Bishop Michael regarded the contemplative religious communities as particularly significant in underpinning the Church's work of intercession, describing them as his own 'spiritual bolsters'. From contemplation flows intercession, and without it intercession is powerless; for the vocation to pray is to put love in where love is not. He described contemplation in a foreword he wrote in 1981 to a book of Mother Mary Clare's teaching, *Encountering the Depths*:

> Contemplation is liberation from our restless brain-activity into the depth of the love of God in our souls, a love, which brings us nearer to the needs of the world around us. It is not a matter of our achieving, but of the opening of our heart to receive the gift which God will pour into it. Christian lives, which know contemplation, will be lives nearer to the love of God in its outflowing stream.

There are two places in his writings where Bishop Michael's understanding of the nature and meaning of intercession emerges with particular clarity and depth. The first is in *Be Still and Know*.[28] Behind what he says lies long meditation upon the language of the psalms, reflection on the meaning of Christ's prayer in St John 17, and on Jesus as the high-priestly intercessor portrayed in the letter to the Hebrews. He emphasizes that in Hebrews the word 'intercede' means 'to be with', or 'to encounter someone'. 'If we think of prayer thus we may find that many aspects of prayer are embraced within the act of being in God's presence.'[29]

> Intercession becomes not the bombarding of God with requests so much as the bringing of our desires within the stream of God's own compassion. Perhaps the theory of intercession may be described in this way. The compassion of God flows ceaselessly towards the world, but it seems to wait upon the co-operation of human wills. This co-operation is partly by God's creatures doing the things that God desires to be done, and partly by prayers, which are also channels of God's compassion.[30]

His second and classic teaching about intercession is found in *The Christian Priest Today*.[31] Here Bishop Michael speaks from the heart and from long experience, as a priest to priests primarily, but also addressing the praying life of the wider Church.

He reflects first on how the disciples learnt to pray simply by being with Jesus and near to him; he taught them as much by example as by word, and so the great prayer of St John 17 'is a kind of summary of the inner meaning of all his prayer, as he gives glory to the Father'.[32] The pattern of his prayer during his human life, recorded in all the gospels, illuminates aspects of his continuing prayer for the Church and for the world. 'He prayed on earth; he goes on praying still', for in the words of the letter to the Hebrews, 'he always lives to make intercession'.[33] This intercession lies at the heart of his relationship with his Father:

> Jesus is with the Father: with him in the intimate response of perfect humanity; with him in the power of Calvary and Easter; with him as one who bears us all upon his heart, our Son of Man, our friend, our priest; with him as our own. That is the continuing intercession of Jesus the high priest.[34]

✳ ✳ ✳

From this flows the vision of Christian intercession: 'We are called to be near to Jesus and with Jesus and in Jesus, to be with God with the people on our heart.'[35] This is the key he believed to the whole mystery of compassionate intercession, and he shows how the sense of being with God leads us to include within the stream of divine love all in whose sorrows we share by our sympathy and concern. 'Being with God with the people on your heart' is the meaning of every act of worship, and supremely of participation in the Eucharist. This vision is kindled and sustained by quiet prayer and worship: 'Be still and know that I am God.'[36] But it flows out into the midst of life and work, for 'anywhere, everywhere, God is to be found. You can be on the Godward side of every human situation; for the Godward side is a part of every human situation.'[37]

To his priests facing the hard slog of Christian ministry over many years ahead, he urged them to think of prayer as simply 'God, myself, and the people – being with Him for them, and with them for Him'.[38] The sense of the prayer of Jesus alongside our prayer sustains this outreach of compassion and intercession. For in this way the divine commandment to love God and to love others is being fulfilled, in a way that is ever more Christlike in its deepening self-sacrifice, and desire to offer forgiveness and reconciliation in costly obedience to the command and example of Jesus himself.

> Your prayer will be a rhythmic movement of all your powers, moving into the divine presence in contemplation, and moving into the needs of the people in intercession. In contemplation you will reach into the peace and stillness of God's eternity, in intercession you will reach into the rough and tumble of the world of time and change.[39]

Towards the very end of his life, Bishop Michael found his days circumscribed by frailty and failing sight, and the inability to read was a bitter blow. For one so mentally active and alert, the increasing powerlessness of old age posed a sharp challenge. Many people found these words, which he wrote at that time, to be of real help in sustaining their own sense of purpose and prayer:

> After immense activity one passes into a phase where passivity is the only way. I pray that you may be finding this passivity as the way in which the soul serves God, not by doing this or that, but by passively receiving the great stream of His love and compassion.[40]

❋ ❋ ❋

He believed that true prayer entailed, however, an active passivity, placing oneself within the divine will, whatever the personal cost. As his contemporary, Dietrich Bonhoeffer, discovered in very different circumstances, there is no Christian discipleship without cost. To pray in this way is to enter deeply, as Bonhoeffer did in Nazi Germany, into solidarity with human suffering and need, and by so doing to engage with evil at its spiritual root. Bishop Michael once said, 'we are not sinning if we are unsure of the answers to hard questions. We are sinning if we do not think or care.' He cared deeply about the tragic moral and spiritual crises of his day, seeing this burden as an inevitable part of the following of Christ:

> His journey to the Father was at every moment a journey deeper and deeper into humanity with its sin, its sorrow and its death. And nowhere was Jesus more utterly within the Father's glory than when in bearing the world's darkness and dereliction on Calvary he cried out that he was bereft of God. Towards heaven, towards the world's darkness; these were but two facets of one journey and one Christ.[41]

Throughout his writings and particularly among his public utterances as archbishop, there ran a constant thread of informed concern for situations where human life was being oppressed by evil: at home, racism and immigration, the rights of prisoners and the future of the death penalty; abroad, apartheid in South Africa, economic development in former colonial countries, human rights abuses in Chile, the ravages of Communism. All these fell within his spiritual purview and exercised his heart and his energies. As leader of a worldwide communion of churches, he was well placed to keep the spotlight on these issues, appealing to both Church and society for a compassionate and principled response. He was not afraid to go into situations of conflict and controversy, for example Northern Ireland or South Africa, and sometimes these meetings upset him profoundly. He always said, for example, that his encounter with President Vorster in 1970 was an encounter with darkness. But he believed that the light of the gospel of Christ had to shine in the darkness, and at times be directed into the darkness, and that Britain and its Church was in a strong position to give a lead.

He was quite independent in his approach, however, and endeavoured to be candid and fair-minded. In attacking apartheid, he did not hesitate to expose racial oppression among the newly independent African countries. Horror at the evil of Nazism did not blind him to the equal and continuing cruelties of Communism, which of course persisted for a much longer period. He himself visited Moscow as Archbishop of York, and his personal sympathy for Orthodox Christianity made him sensitive to the plight of the Church in the Communist lands. This worldwide vision caused him to challenge the self-preoccupation of Western society, too often complacent and blind in its own affluence:

> Christianity teaches us that when we have troubles of our own we see aright when we see them as part of the wider, vaster troubles of mankind as a whole; and when we remember that there are parts of the world where sufferings are so great that our own can scarcely be called sufferings at all.[42]

* * *

This compassionate vision can only happen when the heart is truly open to God in prayer, willing to be enlarged in the love and service of Christ, and sympathy for others. In words of Mother Mary Clare: 'Today we can easily become paralysed by a sense that there is nothing we can do in the face of so much suffering, such lack of love and justice in man's relationship with man; but the Cross of Christ stands at the heart of it all, and the prayer of Christ, now as always, is the answer to human need.'[43]

Sharing in the prayer of Christ, Bishop Michael sensed the pain and cost of this spiritual conflict with evil for the sake of humanity; at times it appeared etched on his face as a result of much agony of heart, for the problem of suffering grows harder to bear as Christian life develops. Reflecting on the Perugino painting of the crucifixion of Jesus, which always hung prominently in his study and which was dear to him, he said:

> Christianity makes a kind of twofold attack on suffering in the world. The Christian will hate the sight of suffering in other people and do his utmost to free them from it. So Christians throw themselves into care for those who suffer in every way they can: the sick, the homeless, the hungry, and those who face persecution, injustice, or abominations like torture. But sometimes when suffering comes to a person and cannot be escaped, the Christian is called upon, in the spirit of Christ, to use it, transformed by patience, love, sympathy, power – like Perugino's picture. Someone said that Christ fought suffering in other people as if nothing could be made of it, but when it came to him he used it as if everything could be made of it.[44]

Bishop Michael identified strongly with those who suffered martyrdom for their faith, and not just Christians, paying sincere tribute, for example, to the memory of Gandhi.[45] Perhaps he sensed that the horrors of the twentieth century were counterbalanced in some mysterious way by widespread martyrdom throughout the worldwide Church. For the twentieth century will always be remembered as the greatest century of Christian martyrdom since the third century. Indeed the 'red' martyrdom of actual death and the inner 'white' martyrdom of spiritual suffering and self-sacrificial compassion are parts of a single divine process within human nature, redeeming it from evil. Who is not to say that the relatively peaceful end of both apartheid and Communism at the end of the twentieth century did not owe much in a hidden way to those on all sides who were prepared to follow Christ's way of non-violent resistance, of moral and spiritual opposition rooted in prayer? To this approach, Bishop Michael certainly gave leadership and encouragement at home and abroad. He once confided that the martyrdom of St Thomas Becket in 1170 in Canterbury Cathedral only really made sense to him once he himself became Archbishop of Canterbury. Preaching to mark the 800th anniversary of this event, he said:

> The martyr speaks to us all. To all of us martyrdom says that we are called as Christians to be loyal: loyal to our faith in the supernatural, loyal to our divine Lord and Saviour, loyal to the saving power of his Cross. We are called fearlessly to uphold what is right amidst the needs of the times in which we are living. And martyrdom also tells us that in the upholding of what is right, self-sacrifice can win victories, which violence and controversy can never win. Hard as it is to grasp, and hard at times to apply in practice to particular circumstances, the way of the Cross is the way in which evil is conquered.[46]

Part Two:
The Primacy of Worship

4

The Saints' Hidden Life

Lord, grant that my faith may become complete, flaming and
tranquil,
To pierce deeply and speak simply in Thy Spirit.
May I apprehend Thee as Light
Lighting every person, every creature, every moment.
May I know Thee as Truth, hearing Thy voice;
That I may serve Thee as Love, loving my brethren,
Asking for no reward, no place, seeking only to lean on Thee.

*

'What have you which you have not received?'[1] These words of
St Paul, which haunted St Augustine, fired Bishop Michael's
insistence upon the importance of relating to the spiritual tradition of the Church and its saints. This emphasis seemed to grow
stronger in the closing years of his life, as he endeavoured to
remind Anglicans and others of the significance of their inheritance. He lamented the popular assertion of 'the pastness of the
past', which is often used by theologians and others in education
and the media to dismantle any sense of a living tradition and
spiritual authority within the life of the Church or society. One
of his favourite phrases described Christianity as being 'a living
past in a living present' – the sense, cultivated by prayer and
study, of the communion of saints, and of the English saints in
particular. He believed that without this, Anglicanism could
quickly lose its spiritual identity and confidence; for Anglican
Christianity is rooted in a historical approach to the gospel as it
is enshrined in the Bible and expounded by the fathers. This has
always constituted the classical Anglican appeal to scripture,
tradition and reason. Those spiritual writers and saints to whom
he made special and repeated reference illuminate what was distinctive about his own spiritual approach and authority. Once

again the seeds of his theological understanding of their legacy lie embedded in *The Gospel and the Catholic Church*.

Throughout this his first book there is a steady emphasis upon the spiritual unity of the Church, and the continuity of its spiritual experience through many generations of Christians. 'From the deeds of Jesus in the flesh there springs a society, which is one in its continuous life.'[2] Modern Christians and their churches need to see their own experience 'as a part of the one life of the one family in every age and place'. This awareness, experienced supremely in the Eucharist, brings to an end self-assertion or complacency by any one part of the Christian tradition. His insight was indeed prophetic, for it has been a remarkable feature of Christianity in the later part of the twentieth century, that the rich resources of many and varied strands of Christian experience have become widely available and appropriated within the life of churches throughout the world. Many Christians are growing up with an eclectic ecumenical experience of worship and thought, less determined by denominational self-consciousness. 'By his place in the body the Christian finds the gospel of the death and resurrection active around and through him',[3] for the body of Christ is larger and deeper than any one institutional Christian church.

Reflecting on the spiritual testimony of St Paul in 2 Corinthians, which is the fountainhead of all Christian spiritual writing, Bishop Michael identified prayerful sympathy between Christians as the decisive hallmark of the Church's true life and hidden unity:

> This unity in pain is very significant – it is the unity of one single organism in joy and sorrow. Suffering in one Christian may beget life and comfort in Christians elsewhere. 'So then death works in us, but life in you.' Thus the sorrows of a Christian in one place may be all-powerful for Christians elsewhere.[4]

* * *

This is pre-eminently true in the life of a saint, who embodies the vocation and the unity of the whole Church. By such travail within a human person, God is at work creating a new humanity: 'The one race exists first: it precedes the local church and is represented by it.'[5] Within the Church the unity of all human beings is being restored, as St Paul declares: 'There is no such thing as Jew and Greek, slave and freeman, male and female; for you are all one in Christ Jesus.'[6] The fact that saints can be discovered in every branch of the Christian Church is a sign that this is true. For example, in the life of St Seraphim of Sarov, who lived in Russia in the early nineteenth century, there is a moment when in a vision he sees the Mother of the Lord, who heals him with these words, 'He is of our race'. There was therefore in the mind of Bishop Michael an indivisible bond, witnessed to by the saints, between unity at the Eucharist, unity among the churches, and unity between human beings of different races and religious traditions.

The work of the saint is to stand, quite often hidden, at the point where God's will for unity conflicts with the sinfulness of human separation. He or she is called to participate in 'the unity that comes to men through the Cross, the eternal unity of God Himself, a unity of love which transcends human utterance and human understanding'.[7] The root of this spiritual vocation lies in baptism, the universal initiation into the kingdom of God, for 'the life of a Christian is a continual response to the fact of his baptism'.[8] What is true of the Church is found to be true therefore also of a saint, who embodies the heart of this Christian vocation: each is defined not in terms of itself, but in terms of Christ whose gospel creates them, and whose life is their indwelling life. The saint does not exist apart from the Church, for 'if we would draw near to the naked facts of Calvary and Easter, we can do so only in the one fellowship whose very meaning is death to self'.[9] This fellowship in suffering is discovered through true prayer that 'looks first at the divine action: for into this divine action the whole of life must by thanksgiving be brought'.[10]

Worship is not merely the act of Christians who gaze upon the action of God; it is rather the act of Christ himself within them. Christ in his body glorifies the Father, and his members share in what he does. The Holy Spirit prays within Christians. It is as though a stream of love flows forth from God to mankind, and returns to God through Christ. Christians cast themselves into this stream; and while their own efforts are called forth in full measure, this stream, which is the essence of worship and prayer, is that of God Himself.[11]

To this vocation all Christians are called, and the reality of this vocation is focused and embodied in the saints, who exist at the heart of the Church's life. Their path is enshrined in the Eucharist wherein Christians discover that which they are called to become, as they receive the Holy Spirit into the heart of their lives, both individually and corporately. There is therefore a golden thread of common spiritual experience running from the time of the first disciples, and through the saints past and present, who by their own prayer, suffering and witness draw people closer to Christ.

> By eating the bread and drinking the cup they will be brought within the death. In an unutterable way they partake of it; it is no longer an event outside them, it becomes something within them to feed and nourish them. ... His dying is become their food.[12]

This place of inner suffering is also a place of prayerful vision, as Christians come to understand the mystery of the Cross, and also 'the whole divine creation whose secrets the crucifixion unlocks'.[13] For in this way the Eucharist mediates the incarnation: both are 'eternal, beyond history, inapprehensible in terms of history alone'.[14] In the words of 2 Peter,[15] Christians are called and enabled to share in the very being of God Himself; or in the words of St Paul, 'Christ within you, the hope of glory to come'.[16] The hidden life and ministry of a saint reveals this to be demonstrably true within fragile human nature, revealing a person transformed by the eternal life which is the gift of Christ's Spirit.

* * *

Bishop Michael frequently emphasized in preaching and in conversation the way in which 'crucifixion, truth, the life of holiness, all these are linked'.[17] The resulting transformation of vision affords insights into the deep mysteries of God, the true wisdom and knowledge that is in Christ alone. Theology cannot be separated from prayer, or from the life of the Church: life, thought and worship are inseparable activities within the body of Christ. The old adage therefore still holds true: '*Lex orandi – lex credendi*' – how we pray determines how we believe. Only as the deformation caused by sin is undone can human persons begin to see clearly, their vision undistorted by sin and self-worship. Hence again the words of the ancient prayer to the Holy Spirit: 'Enable with perpetual light the dullness of our blinded sight.'

Divine wisdom begins at the moment of deepest repentance and compunction, when true understanding of the self in relation to God's utter holiness is glimpsed and never forgotten; and in this way humility is born. Then the whole creation is seen in another light, its sorrows and its secrets, with the Cross as its key, even as St Benedict once saw the whole universe caught up in a single beam of divine light: 'for in thy light shall we see light.'[18] Bishop Michael concluded this about the Church in words that are surely true of individual saints as well:

> It follows that the Church can never be said to have apprehended Truth. Rather it is the Truth as divine action, which apprehends the Church. Dimly it understands what it teaches. … The Church's perilous office of teaching is inseparable from the Church's worship of the mystery whereby it exists.[19]

The reality of the Church's unshakeable if hidden unity stands revealed in individuals and communities, scattered throughout churches and around the world, who embody the values of God's kingdom, men and women and young people being remade in the image and likeness of Christ himself. These vindicate the life-transforming possibilities of Christianity, and the impact of the words: 'Jesus Christ is the same yesterday, today and for ever.'[20] Bishop Michael believed deeply that the Church's unity is 'a unity of race, which can persist beneath all the scandals of outward division. This disturbing situation is a part of the passion of Christ.'[21] Saints are those who have been called and enabled to enter deeply into the pain of that passion, to emerge as hidden beacons of divine light and love, true harbingers of the resurrection. They are the living and life-giving signs of the Church's reality and unity.

This theme is taken up and developed further in *The Glory of God and the Transfiguration of Christ*. Meditating on the saying of Jesus, 'The glory which you gave me I have given to them, that they may be one, as we are one',[22] Bishop Michael identified the meaning of the Church in these words: 'It is the mystery of the participation of men and women in the glory which is Christ's.'[23] These men and women become saints, known and unknown. They experience the tension at the heart of the Church's life between the 'now' and the 'not yet' of spiritual experience, set as they are on the frontier between darkness and light, between human frailty and heavenly vision. 'Here the powers of the age to come are at work within the Church's humiliation. ... This is a doctrine of a Church filled already with glory, yet humbled by the command to await both a glory and a judgement hereafter.'[24] The calling of the individual Christian to this path of living through dying is part of the greater purpose of divine re-creation, whose 'end is a new creation, forged out of the broken pieces of a fallen creation, filled with glory and giving glory to its maker'.[25] These words of Bishop Michael's describe well the reality and significance of the communion of saints at the heart of the Church's life:

> The fellowship of the Church can indeed manifest the glory of God to the consciences of men; but it does so not by providing something for impenitent men to like and admire, but by being a fellowship so filled with God Himself that the conscience is pierced by God's love and judgement. Thus the gospel of the glory of God is always very near to mankind, and yet always very far from them: near, because the divine image is in mankind and the gospel is the true meaning of man; far, because it is heard only by a faith and a repentance which overthrow all man's glorying in himself and his works.[26]

* * *

The Baptism of Jesus and his Transfiguration determine the shape of the gospel story as it moves towards Calvary and the resurrection. This is most evident in St Mark's gospel, but it is also implicit in St John's. Bishop Michael demonstrated this by reference to a sermon[27] of St Leo the Great, who said that the Transfiguration prepared the disciples for the 'humiliation of Christ's voluntary passion by revealing to them the excellence of his hidden dignity'.[28] St Leo asserted that in this mysterious event 'the foundation was also laid of the Church's life, that the whole body of Christ might realize the character of the change which it would have to receive'. From the Orthodox writer, Sergius Bulgakov, Bishop Michael derived the insight that 'what the Baptism is to the public ministry of Jesus, the Transfiguration is to the passion. In both events the Spirit descends'.[29] Close examination of many of the finest saints' lives, for example those of St Columba of Iona, St Francis of Assisi or St Seraphim of Sarov, reveals that this is indeed the hidden structure to their experience of participation in the suffering and the glory of Christ.

Bishop Michael anchored his belief about the meaning of the Transfiguration in the thought of Westcott, the nineteenth-century Anglican scholar whom he greatly admired and to whom he owed much. Westcott said: 'The Transfiguration is the revelation of the potential spirituality of the earthly life in the highest outward form. Such an event, distinct in its teaching from the resurrection, and yet closely akin to it, calls for more religious recognition than it receives. Here the Lord, as Son of Man, gives the measure of the capacity of humanity, and shows that to which he leads all those who are united with him.'[30] The truth of this statement is vindicated in the transfigured lives of many saints, like Columba, Francis and Seraphim, throughout the Christian centuries. They reveal the full capacity of human nature; for at the heart of this mystery lies the transfiguration of suffering through compassion, by which men and women are restored to the image and likeness of God Himself.

The words of St Irenaeus of Lyons, which are now found on Bishop Michael's memorial in the cloisters of Canterbury Cathedral, summarize his own vision of this hidden life of sanctity: 'The glory of God is the living man; and the life of man is the vision of God.' He saw a Christian as sharing in Christ's 'sovereignty of self-giving, pain-bearing love', willing to mount with him the 'throne of Calvary'. This entering into the 'deep darkness of a sinful world' reveals the challenge of goodness confronting the problem of evil. In *Freedom, Faith and the Future,* he concluded that, 'it is the darkness of Calvary and the light of Easter which are still the conditions of the Christian life',[31] and it was his simple but firm belief that 'every act of unselfish love anticipates heaven'.[32] Elsewhere he affirmed that 'it is only through the facing of dark nights, whether in the mystery of God or in the agonies of the world, that the deepening of faith is realised'.[33] This conviction forms the basis of his own definition of what constitutes a saint, which he gave in a sermon he preached in 1973; it unwittingly paints a very credible self-portrait:

> The saint is one who has a strange nearness to God and makes God real and near to other people. ... His virtues do not make him proud, for he is reaching out towards a perfection far beyond them and is humbled by this quest. His sins and failings, which may be many and bitter, do not cast him down, for the divine forgiveness humbles him and humbles him again. He shares and bears the griefs of his fellows, and he feels the world's pain with a heightened sensitivity; but with that sensitivity he has an inner serenity of an unearthly kind, which brings peace and healing to other people. This strange blending of humility, sorrow and joy is the mark of a saint; and through him God is real and near.[34]

✳ ✳ ✳

Towards the end of his last book, *Be Still and Know*, Bishop Michael devoted a whole chapter to explaining his understanding of the communion of saints.[35] Holiness he defined as union with Christ, and communion as participation in the body of Christ. 'Inevitably the theme of holiness and the theme of participation interpenetrate, for the Holy Spirit in making the believers holy lifts them out of their isolation so that to share in the Spirit is to share in one another also'.[36] He believed that 'deep renewal is needed if the communion of saints is to be realized in its ancient meaning and power'.[37] One of the keys to this renewal lay in the Orthodox insight that 'in the family of Jesus all pray for all, and all ask for the prayers of all amidst the unique glory of Jesus'.[38] In this prayer the role of Mary, the Mother of the Lord, is central, for she 'has helped in the creation of the communion of saints' and 'she leads our praises to God'.

His eloquent conclusion to this book is a meditation on famous words of St Augustine from the end of his *City of God*, to which Bishop Michael often returned in the closing years of his life, at retreats and in private: 'We shall rest and we shall see, we shall see and we shall love, we shall love and we shall praise, in the end which is no end.'[39]

> The renewal of the Church will mean, indeed there are signs that it does already mean, a rest which is exposed to the darkness and light of contemplation, a seeing of both the heavenly perspective and the distresses of the world, a loving which passes into costly service, and a praising which is from the depths of the soul.[40]

The roots of Bishop Michael's own understanding of sanctity lay in long and profound meditation upon the teaching of the early Church fathers. His own copies of their writings were closely annotated, reflecting detailed examination on many occasions over the years. Certain key patristic texts were seldom far from his mind as he wrote and spoke, and he was adamant that Christians, and particularly priests, needed greater familiarity with these roots of their belief.

He was cautious, however, about the burgeoning interest in 'spirituality' that was becoming fashionable in the closing years of his life. He sensed that the wrong kind of familiarity could prove to be a barrier to really penetrating the spirit and the teaching of the saints. The fruit of their lives grew only through the sharp pain of self-sacrifice and penitence: could it really be appropriated today without similar personal cost? Moreover, could a saint truly be understood without patient application to historical study, which would place the person in their true context? His own approach was eclectic, and certainly ecumenical; but despite his own scholarly sympathy and interest, he never pursued an academic study in this area as such. For him, it seems, familiarity with the writings of the fathers nurtured his own prayers, and sustained his vision as a Christian pastor and teacher.

* * *

It is fascinating to trace the roots of many of the most distinctive features of his spiritual teaching in the way he refers to the fathers in his writings. He saw himself within a long Anglican tradition, going back through the Tractarians to the Caroline divines of the sixteenth century, to Lancelot Andrewes and Richard Hooker. Bishop Michael firmly believed, and often declared, that there was a distinctively Anglican approach to patristic studies, which was vital to the well-being of Anglicanism, but which was also relevant within the wider life of the Church. His own confidence here was encouraged by a lively sympathy for the Catholic Modernists, notably L'Abbé Loisy, whose brief heyday was in the opening decades of the twentieth century, before being suppressed by the Vatican.

Permeating this approach was a profound belief in Christian humanism. In one of his most lucid studies, *Sacred and Secular*, published in 1965 while he was Archbishop of Canterbury, he examined the relationships between 'the other-worldly and this-worldly aspects of Christianity' – the description comes from the subtitle of these lectures. The foundations of this Christian humanism, which formed and sustained early European civiliz-ation, lay in St Augustine's *City of God* and Dante's *Divine Comedy*. For St Augustine, the invisible Church of God is found to be in the world, but not of the world, its influence calling out the good in men and women and leading them to their eternal destiny. The Christian vision of the world is therefore not a dual-ism, rather a duality where the eternal permeates but at the same time transcends earthly existence. Dante shows in his great poem a profound reverence for man and for nature, 'an observation of human life, acute, sympathetic, and penetrating'.[41] The Renaissance, which had its beginnings in this late medieval vision of God and the world, was initially another manifestation of Christian humanism, embracing both the older theological beliefs and the new discoveries of science and history: its initial Christian roots lay in a profound theology of transfiguration, as can be seen in early Renaissance art.

In the same study, Bishop Michael goes on to examine the nature of asceticism, indicating its true and false forms as either the discipline of nature, or the flight from nature. He asserted that 'true Christian ascesis is rooted in the Bible'.[42] The goodness of the world points beyond itself to the goodness of its Creator; but to perceive and respond to this vision, Christians are called to remain free from the dominance of material things, and from the world of human society with its imperfect values. Those called to the monastic life bear a special witness in a visible way to this vocation to love God in all things and above all things. In a discussion of St Benedict's *Rule*, Bishop Michael revealed an evident sympathy with its ethos as he evaluated its influence, describing it 'as asceticism reaching near to humanism'.[43] He believed that in the end asceticism and humanism are two sides of the same Christian currency of life. For 'God's creation is good, but the gift must not be loved more than the Giver, in the vision of whom is man's destiny'.[44]

* * *

Another emphasis in Bishop Michael's spiritual teaching concerned the limitations of human language. Here certainly his life of prayer governed his whole approach to the language of theology, and to the controversies that so often mar its pursuit. A good example is to be found further on in *Sacred and Secular*, where he cites with approval words of St Hilary to which he often referred: 'We are compelled to attempt what is unattainable, to climb where we cannot reach, to speak what we cannot utter. Instead of the bare adoration of faith, we are compelled to entrust the deep things of our religion to the perils of human expression.'[45] He discussed the bearing of this conviction upon the whole sense of revelation. True to the spirit of Charles Gore and the *Lux Mundi* tradition of Anglican theology, with which he closely identified, Bishop Michael expressed his confidence that, in the words of Hort, 'every addition to truth becomes an opportunity for adoration'.[46] He was not in any way sceptical about the value or power of theological language, simply mindful of its inherent limitations, and of the danger of separating thought from prayer.

He condemned throughout his life any form of narrow rationalism: 'Such a rationalism, alike among the orthodox and the liberal, can miss the way to God by following the false path of a theological science without silence, without penitence, without

contemplation, without wonder.'[47] When asked how this applied
to the language of prayer, he used to reply that prayer could
never be utterly wordless, but that it would often transcend
words. Inspired words can help us begin to apprehend what we
can never fully comprehend about God. But then, as he often
pointed out with a smile, this was also true of words in the best
of human relationships as well. Faith seeks understanding, but
part of faith is trust, and this lays the basis for the language of
love informing both prayer and thought.

This language of love is fundamental to the whole way in
which Bishop Michael sought to unite thought and prayer in
theology. Reflecting on the significance of the famous words of St
Augustine in his *Confessions*, 'Late have I loved thee, Beauty so
old, yet ever new',[48] he wrote eloquently about the inner longing
for God:

> In the very acknowledgement of weakness, inadequacy, inabil-
> ity to pray there is a deepening longing for God. A person
> wants God very much, he is hungry and thirsty for God, and
> perhaps all he is able to tell God is that he has a hunger and a
> thirst for him, though even that is very feeble; but he wishes
> that it were more. And this longing for God when released in
> simplicity appears to be, not something the brain is doing, but
> rather something in the depths of the person. This hungry
> longing for God leads on to an experience in which the self,
> emptying itself of its own capacities, finds itself filled by God.[49]

He goes on to show how in certain saints, a creative balance was
struck between the contemplative vocation of prayer and the
active commitment to prayerful service of others. He believed
from personal experience that there is a 'coming and going'
between these two sides of being Christian, in individual lives and
also in the common life of the Church. The teaching of St Benedict
in his *Rule* achieved this balance; so too did the life of St Gregory
the Great, the apostle of the English, who described St Benedict's
spiritual life in his *Dialogues*. Bishop Michael identified with St
Gregory's sense of the fragility and imperfection of spiritual
vision, and approved of the way in which an ethical emphasis ran
throughout all that Gregory wrote. He read his *Pastoral Rule* as

preparation for his own consecration as a bishop, and quoted with evident sympathy these words of St Gregory:

> Holy men go forth as lightnings when they come forth from the retirement of contemplation to the public life of employment. They are sent and they go, when from the secrecy of inward meditation they spread forth into the wide space of active life. But after the outward works, which they perform, they always return to the bosom of contemplation, there to revive the flame of their zeal and to glow as it were from the touch of heavenly brightness. For they would freeze too speedily amid their outward works, good though they are, did they not constantly return with anxious earnestness to the fire of contemplation.[50]

Like his great and beloved predecessor, St Anselm, Bishop Michael entered his duties from an inner fastness of prayer and contemplation, and his own 'anxious earnestness' to return was seldom absent for long. At the end of *Sacred and Secular*, he identified these three hallmarks of Christian spiritual life: a deep reverence for human persons destined for eternal life; a heavenly serenity able to draw out the sting of suffering; and the humility of a person who has encountered the living God, and who has a lively sense of His presence.[51]

* * *

There is an important chapter in *The Gospel and the Catholic Church*, which examines the teaching of the fathers, and pursues some themes central to Bishop Michael's subsequent spiritual teaching.[52] He takes as his starting point the mysterious words of St Paul writing to the Colossians about 'making up what is left behind of the sufferings of Christ for his body's sake, which is the Church'.[53] The meaning of these words is disclosed in the lives of saints, and in the teaching of the Fathers, eastern and western. 'The close relationship between the doctrines of the body and of redemption is apparent in all the important teaching about the Church from St Paul to St Augustine.'[54]

For St Ignatius, the martyred bishop of Antioch, the unity of the Church rests upon the one life once offered of Jesus himself, and the sharing of Christians in his life and death. In the writings of St Irenaeus of Lyons, another martyr, the goal of God in Christ is the 'recapitulation' of all things through the redemption of humanity. Of this the worldwide spread of the one Church is the pre-eminent sign. At the heart of St Athanasius' struggle against Arianism lay his belief in the essential unity between Christ and his people: Christians become part of the humanity of Christ: 'The Son of God became man, so that the sons of men ... might become sons of God.'[55] In the mind of St Hilary the unity of Christians was a given fact, rooted in the relationship between Jesus and his Father, as he expressed it his prayer in St John 17. St Cyril of Alexandria asserted that 'all mankind is in Christ, since Christ is man'.[56] This is the foundation of a truly Christian humanism; and the social teaching of St John Chrysostom articulates this vision, when he speaks of the 'other altar composed of the very members of Christ; this very body of the Lord is made your altar. ... When you see a poor brother, reflect that you behold there an altar.'[57]

Bishop Michael noted that the ethos of Greek theology was conservative and spiritual, but with an acute sense of the ethical implications of human redemption. It saw the Church as an organism united in its essence to Christ, and understood the word 'catholic' to embrace the whole outward life of the Church, while also describing the inner wholeness of the human person as part of the body of Christ. From this vision sprang the veneration of saints, 'the giving of glory to Christ in his one body, whose family life, seen and unseen, is a manifestation of Christ's own life. ... In reverencing a saint, people reverence the life of Christ who is the life of them all.' Thus the Virgin Mary is the first of those whose human nature was fully indwelt by God: 'one who is humanity indwelt by God, herself the first-fruits of the Church, in whom is focused uniquely in history the truth about the whole body of Christ.'[58] Another way of expressing this would be to say that in the transfigured person of the saint the invisible reality of the Holy Spirit has become incarnate by grace, even as in Christ God was incarnate by nature.

Bishop Michael's sympathy with the Greek fathers is evident here, and remained fundamental throughout his life. But his consideration of the Latin fathers was no less prescient, and indicative of what he was looking for at this early stage of his ministry as a priest and teacher. He approved of St Cyprian's teaching about episcopacy representing the essential unity of the Church, with the important corollary that all bishops are equal.[59] Cyprian's famous assertion that, 'he can no longer have God for a Father who has not the Church for a Mother', embodies a deep sense of the Church as 'the indivisible home of love'.[60] For this sense of the Church's inner loving nature Bishop Michael stood sincerely throughout his years as a bishop, and his home exuded its reality.

✳ ✳ ✳

The same note in the teaching of St Augustine is also strongly emphasized: 'He does not possess the love of God who does not love the unity of the Church.'[61] After some careful discussion of St Augustine's approach towards disruptions to Church unity, Bishop Michael concluded that, 'he thought of the Church as an invisible body, the company of the elect, a reality of which the Church's visible order can be only a faint copy'.[62] Living with the tension between the Church as it now appears, and intimations of the Church as it will be, ran throughout Bishop Michael's experience as a priest and bishop, ordained, as he believed himself to be to serve as a priest of the Church of God within the Church of England. He knew from his own experience, as did St Augustine, that the actual bond between these two manifestations of the Church lay in its long history of persecution and humiliation.[63]

The heart of St Augustine's vision of God lay in his conviction that Christians are caught up within the love of God Himself revealed in Jesus and made real through the Spirit. The mystery of the Eucharist enshrines this dynamic reality: 'The mystery of yourselves is laid upon the table of the Lord; the mystery of yourselves you receive.'[64] This is Bishop Michael's interesting verdict on the spiritual significance of St Augustine: 'He was creative because he had himself been created by Christ in his Church. He became what he became through Christ who converted him, and through the body in which he learned and prayed, and in the

Pauline sense, died and lived.'[65] The parallel with St Paul is significant, for both men pioneered the spiritual language by which the experience of being in Christ could be expressed, revealing within themselves through their writings how the crucible of divine re-making is a process of living through dying.

Writing many years later as Archbishop of Canterbury in 1969 to address some of the challenges of modern theology, he summed up his belief about the significance of the saints in these words:

> The deepest significance of the past is that it contains reflections of what is eternal. Saintly men and women of any age belong to more than their own era: they transcend it. Therefore openness to heaven is necessary for a Christian. Heaven is the final meaning of man as created in God's own image for lasting fellowship with God. Openness to heaven is realised in the communion of saints in deliberate acts of prayer and worship. But it is realised no less in every act of selflessness, humility or compassion; for such acts are already anticipations of heaven in the here and now.[66]

5

Holy Gifts for Holy People

Come, Spirit of God, with God the Father's love, by Christ's
body and blood;
In the new birth of thine own breath.
Come to cover my littleness and consume my sins,
To direct all my desires and doings;
Come with counsel for my perplexities,
With light from thine everlasting scriptures;
Come to reveal the deep things of God,
And what He hath prepared for them that love Him;
Come with thy prayer into mine.

*

'When the Spirit of truth comes, he will guide you into all the truth';[1] these words of Jesus in St John's gospel were central to Bishop Michael's understanding of the living presence and role of the Holy Spirit in Christian life. He stood consciously within the tradition of Anglican thought, pioneered by Gore and others in *Lux Mundi*,[2] and restated in the volume entitled *Essays Catholic and Critical*, which appeared in 1926. Words from its preface sum up Bishop Michael's approach to theology, and especially towards the work of the Holy Spirit:

The two terms catholic and critical represent principles, habits and tempers of the religious mind, which only reach their maturity in combination. To the first belongs everything in us that acknowledges and adores the one abiding, transcendent, and supremely given reality, God. To the second belongs the exercise of that divinely implanted gift of reason by which we measure, sift, examine, and judge whatever is proposed for our belief, and so establish, deepen, and purify our understanding of the truth of the gospel.[3]

Bishop Michael used to point out in conversation the emphasis of Jesus, who amplified the great commandment from the Old Testament to include loving God 'with all your mind'.[4] His own spirit of intellectual enquiry as a biblical scholar was sustained by a living sense of the Holy Spirit, nurtured by worship and contemplation. He demonstrated the truth that being catholic and being critical 'only reach their maturity in combination'. His guiding principle was his belief in the Holy Spirit, who communicates to Christians through the inspired language of scripture, and through the sacrament of Holy Communion.

The best way to glimpse the fervour with which he used to speak of the Holy Spirit is to read the sermon he preached for Pentecost in Canterbury Cathedral in 1963.[5] He began by defining the experience of the Holy Spirit as the knowledge of God's power within a person or community, 'mighty, but intimate and personal too'. In the New Testament, the impact of this experience was upon the minds and consciences of the disciples, it was not just an ecstatic or emotional phenomenon. 'The effects of God's actions are seen in human behaviour: the actions themselves, in minds, hearts and consciences, are describable, however, in symbol alone.' He then proceeded to expound the symbol of fire, used in the description of the coming of the Holy Spirit on the day of Pentecost.[6]

Fire gives light, and 'the Holy Spirit enables you to see, and to see like a Christian – perceiving things as they really are in the eyes or mind of Jesus, and perceiving people as they really are with the light of Jesus upon them'. Fire gives warmth, and the presence of the Holy Spirit 'means that the very love of God creates in us a love which is both our own and also His within us'. He then proceeds with a penetrating discussion, surely drawing on his own personal experience, of how the fire of the Spirit burns away all that is 'fearful, unloving, selfish, and hard', as God's grace breaks down our hidden inner barriers to His love. 'The Spirit will burn his way through to the core of our being in the ever painful process of disclosure, penitence, and divine forgiveness. Only by such burning can our heart be exposed fully to the warmth, and our mind be exposed fully to the light.' Finally, this experience of the Spirit is not just personal; it is shared within the life of the Christian community, creating that *koinonia* or fellowship of sacrifice and self-giving love, which is its true hall-mark. 'There is no seeing and no warming without burning'; or as he put it at the end of his book *Holy Spirit*:

> It is a costly thing to invoke the Spirit, for the glory of Calvary was the cost of the Spirit's mission and is the cost of the Spirit's renewal. It is in the shadow of the Cross that in any age of history Christians pray: 'Come, thou Holy Paraclete.'[7]

✳ ✳ ✳

Bishop Michael wrote *Holy Spirit* in 1977 after his retirement from being Archbishop of Canterbury, and in response to the demands being felt within all the churches at that time from the charismatic movement. It was also an attempt to keep Christian spirituality close to its historical roots in the New Testament, as he says in his preface.[8] He identified several crucial questions: the characteristic marks of the Spirit's influence on a person's life; how the Spirit works in the wider world as well as in the Church; the reliable signs of the Spirit's presence; and the link between the historical events of the gospel and the development of Christian spirituality.[9]

He begins by examining the role of the Holy Spirit in the Old Testament, the two Hebrew words for 'spirit' – 'wind' and 'breath', and the meaning they disclose. He concludes that they reveal a God 'at once beyond and within' His own creation, always active in revealing Himself in a purposeful way.[10] In the gospel this comes to a climax in the baptism of Jesus when the 'interaction of Sonship and Spirit' gives the distinctive character to his ministry as it unfolds.[11] The key words are identified in the gospels, which reveal this pattern of the Spirit at work in the life and ministry of Jesus: 'authority', 'power' and 'spirit' itself. The presence of the Spirit gave Jesus his sense of closeness to his Father, as witnessed, for example, in his private moments of prayer.[12]

Discussing the overshadowing by the Holy Spirit of the Virgin Mary, Bishop Michael indicates its Old Testament associations – the creation of the world, and the presence of God in His temple.[13] The work of the Spirit is an act of new creation: he is, in the words of the Nicene Creed, 'the Lord and giver of life',

through whom Jesus is able to fulfil his promise to give 'life in all
its fullness'.[14] After an extensive discussion of St Paul's understanding of the Holy Spirit, he emphasizes how in Romans 8, as
also in 1 Peter, the Spirit accomplishes 'the transfiguration of
suffering'.[15]

One of the most decisive consequences of belief in the Holy
Spirit in the New Testament is the emphasis placed upon holiness,
the belief that human beings, made in the image and likeness of
God, can be filled with His Spirit. This too has its roots in the Old
Testament, in the belief that 'the holy God is revealed through
the holy nation'.[16] Christians are called to become God's holy
ones: this is a persistent theme throughout the letters of St Paul
and others. This holiness is the meaning and expression of 'sonship', which is the gift of the Spirit to those who believe in Jesus.
This relationship with God finds its supreme expression in the
use of the word 'Abba – Father' – the prayer of Jesus himself: 'For
all who are led by the Spirit of God are sons of God, receiving the
spirit of adoption, enabling us to cry, "Abba! Father!" The Spirit
affirms to our spirit that we are God's children.' Later in this
passage in Romans 8, St Paul describes how the Spirit prays within Christians, according to the will of God.[17]

The spiritual experience of individual Christians is part of the
wider *koinonia* of the Church's life, which the Holy Spirit
creates. In the New Testament, the word means both 'fellowship'
and 'participation'. Discussing the use of this word in Philippians
2, Bishop Michael shows how 'the fellowship has a divine root,
springing as it does from the incentive of God's love, the mind of
Christ and the fellowship of the Spirit':

> The mind of Christ is defined as that of one who sees his divine
> status as an opportunity not for grasping but for pouring him-
> self out and taking the role of a servant. ... To act divinely is
> not to grasp, but to pour self out; that is the secret of the incar-
> nation, and it is no less the secret of fellowship. Such indeed is
> the Christian way.[18]

'Fellowship', 'body' and 'temple' – these are the great images,
which St Paul uses to convey the mystery of the indwelling of the
Spirit of Christ, and each is rich in Old Testament association

and belief. What is true of the Church becomes also true of each individual Christian in communion with Christ and with other Christians. Each person is called to be a sanctuary in which the Holy Spirit can dwell.[19] This is the significance of the word *ecclesia* – the people of all races whom God has called out to be His own.[20] 'The local community of Christians in any place is the one people of God represented in that place.'[21] Christians are united by their common spiritual birth and by their vocation to holiness: the pledge that this is true is the indwelling of the Holy Spirit in the heart of their lives. 'Fellowship, body, temple, and people of God: in each of these concepts the Holy Spirit is the determining factor.'[22] The sacraments of baptism and the Eucharist express and renew this mystery; and the fruits of God's Spirit are the signs that the gifts of His Spirit are real and life-giving.

✳ ✳ ✳

Bishop Michael takes us more deeply into his own spiritual insight and experience when he talks about the Holy Spirit in St John's gospel. Central to his understanding of how the Spirit is communicated throughout this gospel are the words of Jesus: 'It is the Spirit that gives life; the flesh can achieve nothing; the words I have spoken to you, they are both spirit and life.'[23] This text constitutes 'the heart of Johannine doctrine'.[24] The words of Jesus 'are filled with the Spirit's power and they are life-giving in effect'. It is the genius of this gospel to be able by its language and thought to mediate this reality, and this is in fulfilment of the promise made by Jesus that the Spirit 'will glorify me, for he will take what is mine and make it known to you'.[25]

This giving by the Spirit of the life and truth of Christ is a work of divine 'glory', a key word in this gospel. This appears in another passage that is fundamental to the whole doctrine of the coming of the Holy Spirit in St John's gospel: 'On the last and greatest day of the festival Jesus stood and declared, "If any one is thirsty, let him come to me and drink. Whoever believes in me, as scripture says, 'Streams of living water shall flow from within him.'" He was speaking of the Spirit which believers in him would later receive; for the Spirit had not yet been given, because

Jesus had not yet been glorified.'[26] Of this passage, Bishop Michael wrote:

> In this one sentence we have the key to the Johannine doctrine. Jesus is predicting the gift of the Spirit to the believer, but first he must be glorified by his death on the Cross. Death, Glory, Spirit: that is the sequence.[27]

This is a text central to Christian contemplative spirituality, rooted as it is in the affective language of the psalms and other Old Testament poetry. In many ways it sums up the response and experience of Mary, the Mother of the Lord. She shows us that the call of Jesus, the urgent summons of God's love through him, is open to anyone, for 'God so loved the world',[28] and this Jesus himself demonstrated by his actions and parables. Jesus proclaims himself at this great Jewish festival in the holy city of Jerusalem as the fulfilment of the religious longing of Israel, and by implication of all humanity, as it thirsts for the living God.[29] The summons to drink is the call to receive fully and humbly the eternal life of God given through Jesus: in the end it is an act of irreversible embrace, a choice between life and death. For this life means participation in the life and suffering of Christ, a sharing in the cup of his sorrows and a bearing of his grief and compassion.

As was true for Mary herself,[30] it demands a trust that will find its fullest expression in martyrdom, in one form or another.[31] From the pierced side of Christ flows forth blood and water for the salvation of the world.[32] By taking up the Cross, such suffering, voluntarily accepted for the sake of Christ and in union with his, becomes life-giving – it is transfigured by divine glory. For this gospel teaches that self-giving love is the glory of God revealed in Jesus Christ; and through the self-offering of Christ, the Spirit is given to all who will put their trust in him and receive him.[33] The life given is a share in the suffering love within God Himself, Father, Son and Holy Spirit, and that is why it is eternal. Commenting on the significance of the piercing of Christ on the Cross, Bishop Michael wrote:

> It is hard to doubt that symbolism is present. The water means cleansing, the blood means sacrificial life; and from Christ

crucified, cleansing and sacrificial life – each of them linked with one of the sacraments – flow into the lives of those who believe. Water and blood summarize the life of the Spirit; and the pouring out of the gift is now possible because the hour has come and Christ is glorified.[34]

In a further chapter, the role of the Holy Spirit in the final discourses of this gospel is carefully examined. The closeness of the Spirit to Christ, risen and returning from death, means that by 'receiving the Spirit's ministrations the disciples will know Christ's own presence with them'.[35] The work of the Spirit is 'to teach, witness, and convince; to guide into truth, and to declare what is to come; and every part of this ministry is derived from, and in turn points back to, the historic mission and teaching of Jesus'.[36] The double meaning of the word *Paraclete* conveys the mercy of God: it means 'comforter', but it also means 'advocate' in a situation of trial and conflict. Much in these final discourses is directed to the persecution which the disciples will have to endure in their following of Christ. At the end of the gospel, Jesus breathes on his disciples after his resurrection with the words: 'Receive the Holy Spirit.'[37] His breath is the Spirit, poured out through his dying on the Cross. It is an act of new creation; it is also an act of mission: 'As the mission of Jesus was from the Father, so is the apostles' mission from Jesus; and the Spirit is his no less than the Father's.'[38] It is the message of the fourth gospel that 'the glory of self-giving love in the passion and in the mission of the Paraclete is one with the glory of God before the world began'.[39]

Towards the close of his book, Bishop Michael quoted these words of Metropolitan Ignatias of Latakia to the World Council of Churches in 1968:

Without the Holy Spirit, God is far away, Christ stays in the past, the gospel is simply another organisation, authority is a matter of propaganda, the liturgy is no more than an evolution, and Christian loving is a slave mentality.

But in the Holy Spirit, the cosmos is resurrected and grows with the birth pangs of the kingdom, the risen Christ is there, the gospel is the power of life, the Church shows forth the life

of the Trinity, authority is liberating knowledge, mission is
Pentecost, the liturgy is both renewal and anticipation, and
human action is deified.[40]

Bishop Michael returned to the subject of how Christian spirituality was rooted in the historical events of the Gospel in *Jesus and
the Living Past*.[41] Discussing the significance of the Catholic
Modernists, notably Loisy, he noted that at the heart of their
approach lay a very specific appeal to Christian spiritual experience: to 'the experience of the Catholic Church in the making of
saints, and in the union of human lives to God through the
sacraments.'[42] He indicated how this conviction passed into
Anglicanism early in the twentieth century through the spiritual
influence of Friedrich von Hügel, despite the condemnation of
Catholic Modernism by the Vatican in 1907.

Only the event of the incarnation, as Christian tradition has
always understood it, can account for the distinctive but common
characteristics of Christian spiritual experience across so many
church traditions and ages of history. 'The heart of Christian
spirituality through the ages has been the response to the divine
gift of Jesus. In Jesus the gift is given to us and in Jesus the
response is made; and Jesus is one who died and rose again.'[43]
The words of St Paul ring true at the very beginning of this
central golden thread of Christian spiritual life: 'I have been
crucified with Christ: the life I now live is not my life, but the life
which Christ lives in me; and my present mortal life is lived by
faith in the Son of God, who loved me and gave himself up for
me.'[44] It is the work of the Holy Spirit to bring this experience
about and to sustain the life in Christ. By so doing, 'He creates
fellowship and liberates into joy. His power is derived from the
Cross and resurrection of Jesus, and it is His work to make the
impact of those events continuous.'[45] For in the words of the
writer to Hebrews: 'Jesus Christ is the same yesterday, today and
for ever.'[46]

* * *

Bishop Michael devoted most of his energies as a theologian to
the study of the Bible, and especially of the New Testament, and

his belief in the reality of divine inspiration is perhaps best captured in this quotation from Hoskyns, one of his most influential mentors at Cambridge: 'Can we rescue a word, and discover a universe? Can we study a language, and awake to the Truth? Can we bury ourselves in a lexicon, and arise in the presence of God?'[47] He placed these words at the start of his own penetrating biblical study, *The Glory of God and the Transfiguration of Christ*, and paid generous tribute to Hoskyns' teaching in his chapter on 'The Recovery of the Bible' in *From Gore to Temple*.[48]

His own approach to the Bible was, however, never simply academic. When he preached or read the scripture, his sense of the iconic and poetic nature of its language became apparent, radiant even, in the tone of his voice and through his own use of language. It seemed that the words of the Bible were tongued with fire. His attitude was at once historical and meditative, confident that through the pages of scripture the mind of the Holy Spirit engages the minds and hearts of human beings seeking God in each generation.

The fullest and most considered statement of his understanding of the inspiration of the Bible is in the opening chapter to the 1962 edition of *Peake's Commentary on the Bible*. It is entitled 'The Authority of the Bible', and it was a judicious and characteristic attempt to steer between the Scylla of uncritical fundamentalism, and the Charybdis of scepticism born of fashionable cultural relativism. Both these approaches to the Bible he abhorred, and their blandishments and dogmatism called forth rare moments of utter condemnation in private conversation. His own approach was principally prayerful and historical, and he once said that with hindsight he felt that the study of history was now more appropriate for understanding the Bible than the study of classics, which had been the traditional route in his own generation; much of his own private reading was historical.

This chapter on 'The Authority of the Bible' provides a balanced framework and expression of his thought, and was probably representative of the broad middle ground in Anglican biblical scholarship at the time. He asserts that 'the central fact of Christianity is not a book but a person – Jesus Christ himself, described as the Word of God'. The Bible therefore contains the Word of God, rather than actually being the Word of God: 'The collection of sacred books was not the basis of the belief in a divine revelation, but its consequence.'[49] The historical foundation for this becomes apparent when it is recognized that both Old and New Testaments were significantly formed by oral tradition before finally being written down. The words of scripture are therefore the means of divine communication, not simply a divine communication in themselves. A living divine mind generated their essence through the imperfect languages of human beings, who in each generation were responsive to the Word of God.

The concept of the 'Word of God' is at the heart of the Bible, in both Testaments. In the Hebrew word and thought there is an unbreakable connection between message and event, between saying and thing. The great prophets spoke in the Name of the Lord, their message sprang from a living relationship with God Himself. This is no less true of the historical books in the Old Testament, which were linked to the writings of the prophets, indicating that history could only be interpreted in the light of divine purpose. This belief governs how Christians relate to the Old Testament: 'To the Christian Church these books were God's Word not in its completeness, but as the Word of His promise: their significance lay not in themselves, but in a fulfilment which was beyond them.'

Over the pages of the Old Testament, the earliest Christian Church placed as a filter the sufferings of the servant of the Lord, portrayed in Isaiah 53 and elsewhere in the prophets and the psalms. Thus through the lattice of the Old Testament the face of Him who is the Word of God is disclosed as the suffering face of love. So it is that in the New Testament, 'Jesus Christ and the apostles appealed not only to the text of the scriptures, but to the dynamic history of law and prophecy which lay behind them'.[50] Jesus came to fulfil the Law and the prophets, supremely by his death on the Cross and his resurrection. This transformed how the earliest Jewish Christians handled the Old Testament: 'Living under the new covenant, the Church was able to use the ancient scriptures in the new way which the gospel of Christ had created.'[51] The New Testament is the monument in writing to this metamorphosis. Language was drawn from the tradition of Israel, but it was transformed through the memory of the person of Jesus, and his suffering and death. 'The imagery seems to show Jesus fulfilling the role of Israel in attaining to triumph, but attaining it only through humiliation.'[52]

> There was in Jesus the divine utterance not only in his teaching and message, but also in himself: the Word and the person were utterly one. Furthermore, the Word, who was made flesh, had himself been 'in the beginning with God' at work in the creation of the world, and in the giving of light and life to mankind. Thus, in a sense hard to describe, and faintly yet decisively perceived, the scriptures of the Old Testament not only prepared the way for Christ, but also revealed him, as the Word of God, now incarnate in him, which had been at work from the beginning.[53]

* * *

God's constant purpose of self-revelation through His Word, and of self-giving in Christ, is what gives unity to the Bible: one divine mind of love holds it all together, without diminishing its historical character and diversity. Bishop Michael quotes words of Origen: 'The sacred books were not just the works of men: they were written by inspiration of the Holy Spirit, at the will of the Father of all through Jesus Christ.'[54] In the fathers, divine possession is a common way of explaining the nature of inspiration; but there is also ample emphasis on the role of the human mind and will as well. Modern critical and historical methods have enhanced this sense of the human context of the biblical texts, in all their rich diversity and through many centuries of development. But this has raised for some the vexed question: 'Without the doctrine of verbal inerrancy, how may belief in the divine authority of the Bible be held?'[55]

After outlining the various modern approaches to the Bible in response to this dilemma, Bishop Michael came down firmly in favour of the validity of a strictly historical approach, confident that 'the process of historical enquiry helps us to understand the nature of the authority of the scriptures. Their authority lies in relation to Jesus Christ, who is the Truth.'[56] But history is always a mingling of fact and interpretation, and 'no words, even inspired words, are wholly adequate to convey the reality of God'. A doctrine of verbal inerrancy is therefore ruled out as inadequate to the mystery of God Himself, and of how He communicates to and through human beings in the Bible. Poetry, symbol and art all have their place in the rich panorama of biblical language, indicating the transcendent quality characteristic of divine inspiration and self-communication. The question confronting the reader of the Bible is therefore not so much 'is it true?' but rather 'how is it true?'

> The hearing of the Word in the Bible, and the pursuit of critical study are in no way incompatible. It is necessary to reject the idea that a firm faith implies the repelling from the mind of the questions raised by criticism – for the faith of a Christian is faith in God, and God is the giver of the scholar's quest for truth as he sets out in search of it, as one not knowing whither he goes. It is required of faith that it does not deny the spirit of inquiry; and conversely it is required of the spirit of inquiry that it does not cling to prejudices as to what God can or cannot do in the sovereign activity of his Word.[57]

He concludes this essay on the authority of the Bible with the assertion that 'within the Church of God, word and sacrament interpret each other'. The gospel preached speaks from the past to the present and makes a contemporary impact. Christ himself is present in the sacrament of the Eucharist, and each interprets the other, drawing Christians into the spiritual reality of divine life and love of which the Bible speaks. It is this reciprocal action which has sustained the Church throughout the ages, and which connects it to the experience of Israel. It is the secret at the heart of Christian life – 'Christ within you, the hope of glory to come'.[58]

* * *

Once again *The Gospel and the Catholic Church* reveals the roots of Bishop Michael's belief. In chapter nine, he examines what Christians mean by 'The Truth of God'. The key question he posed was this: 'What is this Truth which has created both the Church and the Bible?'[59] Christians discover that divine truth is received through repentance and thought, moulding belief and life in equal measure. The use of the word 'wisdom' in the New Testament is also highly significant. For St Paul, the wisdom of Christ crucified opens the door to the wisdom of the Spirit.[60] This wisdom is cosmic in scope, for everything gradually becomes intelligible in the light of the crucifixion and resurrection of Christ. Human sin and self-worship prevent the full appreciation of this divine wisdom, however, so repentance becomes the key to truth. Thought and worship become inseparable in the human response to God within the life of the Church:

> In these three ways the Church will be faithful to the biblical meaning of Truth: by reverencing the works of God every-where, and discerning the Spirit of God manifested in the endeavours of human minds; by keeping before itself and before men the scandal of the Cross; and by remembering that orthodoxy means not only correct propositions about God, but the life of the one body of Christ in the due working of all its members.[61]

In his book *The Resurrection of Christ*[62] Bishop Michael returned to the way the language of scripture communicates the supreme miracle of God's grace – the revelation of the resurrection of Christ. His definition of miracle is very perceptive. He points out that although a miracle often appears to interrupt the normal laws of nature and of historical cause and effect, it does so to 'vindicate another and a higher aspect of law'.[63] The miracle of the resurrection reveals a deeper order of being, which is transcendent and eternal, as it 'unveils a new level of glorified human life'. Through the inspired language of the Bible, the Holy Spirit communicates the reality of this vision. Moreover, 'there was in the resurrection a gentleness and a restraint akin to that which was seen in the ministry and passion of Jesus'.[64] This divine restraint governs also the language by which the event was described and its truth conveyed, for it is no part of God's will to force the human mind and heart.

The historical evidence in the gospels provides a context of overwhelming probability to support belief in the resurrection of Christ. The evidence, however, is not in itself proof; but without it the divine reality could never be communicated in a way that could be received with reasonable faith. On the other hand, 'without the resurrection the historian has the problem of Jesus, no less than the problem of the Church, to explain'.[65] The written testimony of the apostles in the New Testament to the risen Christ reflects a new vision of life 'wherein thinking, feeling and action were made creative under this new and unexpected impulse'.[66] This is the root of its inspired and authoritative character, for 'read in its own light, the Bible has the resurrection as its key'.[67]

✻ ✻ ✻

It is in *The Glory of God and the Transfiguration of Christ* that the matter of how biblical language is inspired is most closely and extensively examined. The book revolves around the key word 'glory'. Bishop Michael shows how before the coming of Jesus, the word had already been metamorphosed in translation from Hebrew into the Greek of the Septuagint, so that 'conceptions which are distinct in Hebrew and Aramaic literature became, in the Septuagint, fused into a unified imagery of God's glory and God's dwelling with His people'.[68] The Greek of the Septuagint is the vocabulary of the New Testament, for already in the Greek Old Testament 'the doctrine of the divine glory is presented with a great unity and impressiveness'.[69]

A similar pattern of fusion and metamorphosis may be discerned in the gospels when the concepts of 'the Son of Man' and of 'glory' are brought together in some of the most distinctive teaching of Jesus. Originally, in Daniel 7, the heavenly Son of Man is a figure of divine glory and rule; but 'the novel element in our Lord's use of it is unmistakable: "the Son of Man must suffer." It is by a road of suffering that Jesus must enter into the glory, which the Father has in store for him as Messiah, King and Judge. And side by side with this theme there is the challenge to the disciples: if they will suffer, they too will share in the glory.'[70] Thus in the New Testament 'the use of the word "glory" is renewed in the teaching of the apostolic Church, but meanwhile the event of the resurrection has wrought a decisive change'.[71] The crucifixion of Jesus was the crucible in which this language has been transformed, so that in a new way 'the imagery of glory expresses realities that reach beyond itself. At the centre of these realities is Jesus Christ himself.'[72] This pattern of New Testament language only makes sense with the Cross as its key; and the see-ing of God in Christ crucified 'is the transfiguration of man'.[73] The mystery is that the passion and the glory of Jesus are one, and to be a Christian is to discover that this is so, and to enter thereby into the eternal life of the resurrection.[74]

Discussing the final discourses of St John's gospel concerning the work of the Holy Spirit in glorifying Christ, Bishop Michael drew this conclusion:

> A Trinitarian doctrine of God is here inescapable. It is inescapable as touching the activity of God in history, for the glorifying of the Father by Jesus is perfected only in the glorify-ing of Jesus by the Spirit. It is inescapable as touching the being of God Himself, for the sharing of the Son in all that the Father has is paralleled by the sharing of the Spirit in all that the Son has. The revelation of the glory of God to the disciples involves their coming to perceive that the Spirit is all that the Son is – namely God indeed.[75]

These great discourses in St John's gospel contain many examples of how the inspired language of scripture mediates a pattern of truth accountable for only in the light of Jesus, but at the same time pointing beyond itself to the transcendent reality of God Himself. In the life, ministry, death and resurrection of Christ, the inner truth about God's nature is revealed, and to do justice to this, scriptural language is metamorphosed irreversibly. 'It is by the humiliation of the Son's winning of glory in the toils of history that the eternal glory of the divine self-giving is most fully disclosed.'[76] Bishop Michael then quotes at length some words of Evelyn Underhill about how 'the eternal Godhead utters His word within the human arena and stoops to human nature', revealing His 'inmost nature' in the humanity of Jesus. She indi-cates how 'the real splendour of catholic devotion, its mingling of spaciousness and transcendence with homely love, is missed unless there is a remembrance of that unconditioned glory which enters our conditioned world through that lowly door'.[77]

So if the story of the Transfiguration is 'filled with current messianic ideas, it is not simply the creation of these ideas; for it contains a novel element, drawn from the gospel of Jesus, which disturbs these ideas and recreates them'.[78] The grit of voluntary suffering creates, as it were, the pearl of the resurrection; the Cross metamorphoses the language of divine revelation, as its fullness is revealed in the face of Jesus Christ.[79] It is in this mysterious story of the Transfiguration that all 'the diverse elements in the theology of the New Testament meet': it is the 'mirror in which the Christian mystery is seen in its unity'.[80]

✳ ✳ ✳

For Bishop Michael, the link between the inspired language of the Bible and the reality mediated through the sacrament of the Eucharist was profound and reciprocal in its effect. He believed that the Eucharist is the spiritual crucible in which Christian understanding of the meaning of language is remade, in the sense that it enables a person with heart and mind to participate in the transforming reality of Christ through the power of the Holy Spirit. In this sacrament word interprets action, and action demonstrates that which word describes. There is in scripture and in Holy Communion a dynamic *anamnesis*, or remembering of God's saving acts in the person of Jesus; for as Jesus himself said: 'The words I have spoken to you are both spirit and life.'[81] This solemn *anamnesis* brings the past and the present together within the eternal reality of God, enabling Christians to share in the sacrifice of Christ made once for all upon the Cross, and to receive the life of the resurrection, which flows from his wounded side.

The Eucharist itself is in every aspect a dramatic embodiment of the saving message of the Bible. In the first half of the service there is the proclamation of the purpose of God through the words of scripture, and pre-eminently of the gospel. But all the language of the Eucharist – prayers, creed, consecration – is steeped in the language of the Bible, revealing its hidden pattern of meaning, and providing, as it were, the lantern through which the light of Christ can shine, or the mirror in which his face may be glimpsed. The promise of Jesus from his final discourse confirms that this is the work of the Holy Spirit: 'He will take what is mine and make it known to you.'[82]

Sacramental worship, expressed in the language of scripture, leads to a transformation of the whole person, of vision, sensibility and understanding. This was very evident in the way Bishop Michael celebrated the Eucharist: his sensitivity and silences communicated a strong awareness of the presence of Christ. For the language of the gospel and of the liturgy is the language of love, the opening by which the Holy Spirit comes to pray through human feeling and language offered in worship and self-sacrifice. This is best expressed in words at the heart of the Orthodox Divine Liturgy: 'Thine own, of thine own, for all and through all we offer Thee, O Lord.' In this way, a person is led by the Holy Spirit to the place where worship 'in spirit and in truth'[83] occurs, the inner sanctuary of the heart – a place set apart in awe and mystery.

Set Apart in Awe and Mystery

Lord, thou art present – in thy lowliness, and in thy glory:
Thou that dwellest among us, whom we refused, wounded
and slew;
Thou the immortal victor, the everlasting king.
Thou in thy strength, and in thy tender love:
Thou with thy yielded life, with thy living Spirit;
Lord, thou art here – my Lord and my God.

*

The Eucharist was at the heart of Bishop Michael's spiritual life and teaching. His own devotion and attention while celebrating were exemplary and made a powerful impression. He was not averse to using the modern liturgies,[1] but was probably more comfortable with *The Book of Common Prayer*, and with the earlier stages of liturgical reform couched in traditional language. He deplored, however, the proliferation of pamphlets in divine worship. He handled ceremonial celebrations in the Anglo-Catholic manner with evident enjoyment, but revealed more of his own personal approach in simpler celebrations, including those in his own home. He was not a ritualist, though he was drawn into Anglicanism by the spirit of Anglo-Catholic devotion, which he once described as 'the sense of mystery, and awe, and of another world at once far and near … a sense that we were vividly in the presence of the passion of Jesus, and also vividly near to heaven to which the passion mysteriously belonged, so as to be brought from the past to the present.'[2] Towards the end of his life, attendance at a daily Eucharist became vital for him. The deep influence of the prayer of consecration in *The Book of Common Prayer* is everywhere apparent in his spiritual teaching about the Eucharist.

In *The Gospel and the Catholic Church* it is already evident how his belief in the meaning of the Eucharist was a pivot upon which his whole theology turned: 'The Eucharist sets forth Christ crucified and the one body, and shows the constant relationship between these truths.'[3] It is the outward expression of the message of the New Testament, and it is 'the Church's act of common worship, the outward structure which points beyond men's needs and feelings to the divine sacrifice on the Cross and in heaven, and beyond the individual and the local fellowship to the continuous life of the universal Church'.[4] The chapter in this first book, entitled 'The Liturgy', is seminal,[5] and repays close attention.

Bishop Michael regarded the Eucharist as the key to understanding the gospel; and at the same time he saw how the institution of the Eucharist by Jesus only made sense in the light of the entire New Testament tradition: 'The meaning of his actions is determined by the whole meaning of his life and work; and it is here that the crucial point with regard to the institution of the Eucharist lies. Its interpretation depends on the whole interpretation of his ministry.'[6] Christ's words of institution therefore mediate the reality they describe, and to receive communion is to participate in the life and sacrifice of Christ. For 'his words and actions were his final unfolding of the meaning of his death, and in them the whole meaning and power of that death were present. The disciples were brought into the death: his dying is become their food.'[7] This has a transforming effect upon a person, and upon their vision of God, as the crucifixion and resurrection of Jesus 'unlocks the secrets of the whole divine creation'.[8]

When St Paul challenged the church at Corinth about sharing in food already offered to idols[9] he did so on the assumption that in the Eucharist Christians truly partake of the life of Jesus. This is something given by God, not simply generated by human faith or attitude. To share in the Eucharist is also to share in the life of the one body – the Church.[10] This has a moral dimension, determining the spiritual integrity of the Church's life, as well as the individual's vocation to become the sanctuary of the Holy Spirit: for 'in all Christian thinking about the body, the Eucharist and the Church are inseparable'.[11] Commenting on the discourse which follows the Feeding of the 5000 in St John 6, Bishop Michael said: 'The power to feed and to give life is derived from the Father, and hence the incarnation and the Eucharist reveal the truth about the Father and the Son. Behind the life, the death, the feeding, there is the eternal relation of the Father and the Son, which the life, the death, and the feeding reveal.'[12] So it is that what the Eucharist commemorates points beyond itself to an eternal divine reality: 'The Eucharist is the breaking into history of something eternal, beyond history, inapprehensible in terms of history alone.'[13] History and human life now have their significance in what lies beyond them. It is this divine reality and purpose that governs the way language itself is metamorphosed in sacramental worship. 'Underlying the language there is something greater than the language can express, and something which is creating language, thought and worship.'[14] This determines the whole ethos and atmosphere of the Eucharist – its holiness, and the sense of wonder at the great unknown that lies beyond.

> Just as our Lord, in the awe and isolation of the passion was set apart from mankind so as to be nearer to them by his death, so also the Eucharist had to be set apart from common meals in an awe and mystery, whereby its nearness to the common life was to be realised more deeply. The gospel that moulded the structure of the Church moulded also the form of the Church's worship. This worship was and is the liturgy, the divine action whereby the people of God share in the self-oblation of Christ.[15]

For Christ is the eternal priest: the whole of his life and ministry revealed the profound self-offering within God Himself. His sacrifice, culminating on the Cross, reveals the nature of God as Father, and the cost of His loving sacrifice made once for all in human history. 'His presence in heaven is as a sacrifice, and in the Eucharist his presence cannot be otherwise. He is there as the one who gave himself on the Cross, and who there and then unites his people to his own self-giving to the Father in heaven. Christ's unique act in history is the source of what Christians do.'[16] This is also the message of the letter to the Hebrews, and it governs the way in which the Church later used priestly and sacrificial language in relation to the Eucharist. This celebration of the sacrifice of Calvary reaches out beyond the life of the

Church to embrace the world in all its pain. For in contemplating the mystery of the Eucharist, men and women look upon him whom they have pierced,[17] and find in the life-giving action of Christ the redemption and meaning of human life and suffering. All Christian prayer finds its focus here, as every part of life is drawn into self-offering in union with Christ's and with that of his Church. 'The Christian does not share in the liturgy in order to live aright; he lives aright in order to share in the liturgy.'[18]

A similar pattern may be discerned in the prayer of Jesus in St John 17, to which Bishop Michael gave special attention in *The Glory of God and the Transfiguration of Christ*, as well as elsewhere in his preaching and writing. This he believed provides the spiritual context for the institution of the Last Supper. 'Jesus speaks to the Father as the Father's eternal Son, and yet he speaks from the midst of a historical crisis of human flesh and blood.'[19] He regarded it as enshrining Christ's own prayer of self-consecration, a view he derived from Hoskyns and, before him, Westcott. Its theme is *Christus Victor*, though the price of that victory is expiation for sin through death on the Cross. The disciples represent the whole of humanity, which falls within the redeeming love and authority of the Son.[20] The key words are: 'Consecrate them by the truth.'[21] The Cross reveals the truth that human sanctification rests upon Christ's own consecration of himself for them, and the Eucharist mediates this sanctification. St John's account of the passion of Jesus reveals how 'the prayer is being answered and the Son is being glorified'.[22] This is also true of the shape and content of the Eucharist: it retraces the suffering footsteps of Christ as he mounts the throne of his glory, which is the Cross. The whole drama of incarnation and redemption is set forth for adoration and participation. This is the mystery that lies at the heart of the Church's mission, by which God's judgement and glory in the face of Jesus Christ are made known to all humanity.

* * *

Bishop Michael was a conscious heir to the rich tradition of Tractarian thought and spirituality to which he often returned. This he had made his own as an undergraduate at Cambridge, and it was deepened by his time at Cuddesdon, a place redolent of great spiritual figures like Charles Gore, and Edward King, the saintly bishop of Lincoln. In his book, *From Gore to Temple*, he acknowledged this debt, not least in relation to his own understanding of the Eucharist. Of Gore and his contemporaries he wrote: 'To all of them the Eucharist was a constant interpreter of doctrine, and the Eucharist enabled them to see the doctrine in terms cosmic and liturgical, no less than evangelical.'[23] The heavenly priesthood of Jesus was central to this vision, and they understood the shed blood of Christ to signify not just his death but also 'the life that has passed through death'.[24] His sacrifice is at once living and life-giving.

Gore's teaching culminated in the belief that sacrifice is only perfected in communion. Our offering is joined to that of Christ in heaven and so becomes the bread of heaven; but at the same time Christ's sacrifice is presented to God in the Eucharist by those who seek the Father's presence. Bishop Michael drew special attention to the view of Spens in the volume of essays *Catholic and Critical*, published in 1926: 'Every Eucharist, like the Last Supper, invests our Lord's death with a sacrificial significance, so that the one unrepeatable fact of Calvary is kept at the heart of our approach to God.' This Anglican tradition found expression in the lovely words of William Bright's hymn: 'Look, Father, look on His anointed face, and only look on us as found in Him.'[25] Later in this book, Bishop Michael quotes with evident approval the way in which Gore spoke of the Church as 'an extension of the incarnation'. He noted how this approach had its root in the way a much earlier Anglican divine, Jeremy Taylor, had spoken of the Eucharist. Gore said, 'The Spirit is the life-giver, but the life with which he works in the Church is the life of the Incarnate one, the life of Jesus.'[26] Bishop Michael concluded his consideration of the Eucharist in this book by reviewing the report *Doctrine in the Church of England*, started in 1922 but only completed in 1937, whose words on this point he cited:

> If the Eucharist is spoken of as a sacrifice, it must be understood as a sacrifice in which we do not offer Christ, but where Christ unites us with Himself in the self-offering of the life that was 'obedient unto death, even the death of the Cross.'[27]

The pastoral implications of how the Eucharist is celebrated at the heart of the Church's life were seldom far from his thoughts. In his first book, *The Gospel and the Catholic Church*, he showed himself fully aware of the first stirrings of what became the Parish Communion movement after the war, but which at the time he was writing in the 1930s had its early manifestation in continental Catholicism.[28] His sympathy and interest were evident, but in a famous address while Bishop of Durham he warned against some of the dangers inherent in making the parish communion the central and normal act of worship in Anglican churches. He could see its benefits, uniting different traditions of churchmanship and making communion more accessible to more people. But the price too often paid was a familiarity with the sacrament and a shallowness of teaching, which destroyed the sense of reverence that he felt was appropriate and indispensable to eucharistic worship. Because Anglicans were 'at one in believing our Lord's sacrifice to be the great fact under whose shadow we worship', there should be more care in the way in which the sense and meaning of that sacrifice was taught and cultivated. 'The awe in the individual's approach to Holy Communion, which characterized both the Tractarians and the Evangelicals of old, stands in contrast to the ease with which our congregations come tripping to the altar week by week.'[29] His words have proved prophetic.

He challenged this ease of approach to Holy Communion throughout his life, urging people to remember that 'the reception of communion is dreadful as well as precious', and that clergy are called not simply to generate communicants, but to prepare people for union with Christ through the hard road of prayer and penitence, which is the only true approach to Holy Communion. A superficial sense of church community did not necessarily constitute *koinonia* or true Christian fellowship, and was no substitute for the 'participation in Him, by which we have our deepest togetherness with one another'.[30] Nor did he think it appropriate to concentrate all energy on a single main celebration at the expense of other types of services, and especially of the tradition of early morning Holy Communion. He valued this particularly, for 'it keeps alive, and gives real place to, the meditative element in religion'.[31] He remained confident none the less that the revival of the Eucharist as the normal and central service throughout the Anglican and Roman Communions was full of promise. The growing similarity between their rites, based on careful liturgical scholarship, could hold a key to the deepening renewal of spiritual life and ecumenical unity.

> In the long run, the Eucharist will be its own interpreter and teacher. For the supreme question is not what we make of the Eucharist, but what the Eucharist is making of us, as together with the Word of God it fashions us into the way of Christ.[32]

Hints of his own experience of this peep through in the addresses he gave to his priests on the eve of their ordination, published as *The Christian Priest Today*. Describing the priest as a person of the Eucharist, he says: 'He finds that at the altar he is drawn terribly and wonderfully near not only to the benefits of Christ's redemption but to the redemptive act itself.'[33] The priest is called to 'help the people realise both the God-ward and the man-ward aspects of the liturgy. He will show them that they too are brought near to the awful reality of the death of the Lord on Calvary as well as to his heavenly glory.' In doing this, the priest 'is drawn closer to Christ's own priesthood than words can ever tell'.[34]

✳ ✳ ✳

True worship is human response to God's initiative, and this axiom lay at the root of all Bishop Michael's teaching about the primacy of worship in the Christian life. 'He who prays looks first at this divine action; for it is *there* that prayer starts, and not with human needs and human feelings; and into this divine action the whole of life must, by thanksgiving, be brought.'[35] The paradox of the incarnation is that the drawing near of God in love and tenderness, supremely revealed in the manger and on the Cross, 'brings a sense of awe before One whose love and wrath are past all comprehension'.[36] To pray is therefore to stand on the edge of the abyss of God's power and love.

To worship is to fulfil the destiny of human nature and existence; this is the vision of the Old Testament whereby 'creation becomes articulate in and through man'.[37] But 'the perfect act of worship is seen only in the Son of Man', glorified upon the mountain, but also glorified upon the Cross.[38] Into this worship Christians are called, uniting their prayers with those of their head. The light of Calvary and Easter interprets the meaning of the life and ministry of Jesus; it illuminates also the life of the Church today, and the meaning of Christian spiritual experience and prayer. The nearness and the awesome mystery of God revealed in Christ draw all who seek Him deeper into this divine movement of worship and love, which is the very heart of God the Trinity.

Spirituality is therefore inseparable from prayer and worship, and it is expressed in Christian fellowship and service.[39] As William Temple once said: 'It is sometimes supposed that conduct is primary, and worship tests it. That is incorrect: the truth is that worship is primary, and conduct tests it.'[40] In a penetrating critique, entitled 'Christian Spirituality and the Modern World', delivered to an ecumenical gathering at the University of Louvain, Bishop Michael outlined what he perceived to be the modern threats to Christian spiritual life: the alliance of technology and hedonism, and the false confidence it induces; the whirl of life in the present, with the mind so overcrowded by information and stimuli as to be incapable of reflective thought; and the deep inner fear induced by 'the loss of touch with God', of which sexual preoccupation and drug abuse are symptoms.

> It is when the Creator is forgotten that His gifts and creatures are allowed to dominate and to become ends in themselves. So it is that technology, or money, or comfort, or sex can rule man, instead of having their true place, which is to be ruled by man for the glory of God. So we have a society where man, apparently mature in his powers of mind and spirit, loses his freedom and his way to God.[41]

This malaise, which lurks at the root of all human unhappiness and disorder, is an estrangement from God, and a loss of the sense of His reality. This is the tragedy of the modern age in particular, and in response to it Christians are called 'to witness to the reality of God Himself. They do so by the depth of their communion with Him, and by their humility before Him. The unknown writer of the epistle to Diognetus said, "As the soul is to the body, so are Christians in the world." Christians serve a world which has lost its soul by the lifting up of their own souls in adoration.'[42] But as in St John's gospel, this 'lifting up' means taking up the Cross of Christ in response to God's own self-giving in Jesus.

This is why contemplative prayer is vital for the Church's witness as well as for individual spiritual life. Such costly prayer must suffuse the liturgical life of the Church, for 'without meditative and contemplative prayer the sacramental life can become shallow and formal, and lack interior depth'.[43] This type of prayer is accessible to any Christian, but it requires 'a will for leisure and passivity in the midst of ceaseless activity'. It thus challenges directly many modern perceptions and priorities of life. Contemplative prayer is, however, the vital key to experiencing the reality of the Church's spiritual unity, and to 'the recovery of the inner soul of Christendom'.[44]

One of Bishop Michael's favourite texts for a retreat were words already quoted of St Augustine: 'We shall rest and we shall see; we shall see and we shall love; we shall love and we shall praise, in the end that is no end.'[45] There is a fine exposition of its meaning in an address entitled 'Heaven and Hell', delivered at New College, in London in 1960.[46] He believed that heaven 'will be a perfection in which the contradictions familiar in our present existence are resolved'. These he identified as the oscillation between possession and discovery, rest and action, worship and service. Only in God's will is our peace, when 'all our familiar contradictions disappear in the glory of God'.[47]

> Wherever there are works in which God is present through the humility and charity of the doer, heaven is not far off. Wherever there is the prayer of a soul hungry for God, and ready amidst its own weakness and failure to be filled with God's charity, heaven is very near.[48]

* * *

Bishop Michael drew deeply upon Christian mystical theology, and although he seldom spoke directly of his own inner spiritual experience, the way he wrote about the mystics with whom he felt a rapport is illuminating. He devoted a whole chapter to this subject in *Sacred and Secular*, his Scott Holland lectures of 1964. He identified the promise of Jesus in his final discourse as a key text: 'We will come to him and make our dwelling with him.'[49] No less important is St Paul's personal testimony to mystical experience in his second letter to the Corinthians;[50] here suffering is the concomitant of vision. These texts are the New Testament anchors of later Christian mysticism.

Bishop Michael repudiated completely the Protestant critique that there is no place for mysticism in Christianity, endorsing instead the remarkable study of St Augustine's spiritual theology by John Burnaby, called *Amor Dei*.[51] He denied, however, that mysticism was about the soul climbing up to God, or trying to possess Him. 'It has to be noticed that in mystical experience the supreme moment is one of passivity. It is when the mind seems to cease to think, and the powers of the self seem to cease to function, that God gives what He alone can give; and God possesses the soul far more than the soul possesses God.'[52] This insistence upon passivity runs throughout his teaching, and is the more remarkable considering his own temperament and mental restlessness. He accepted that to some extent Christian mysticism may have drawn on pre-Christian sources, but asserted that these elements were transformed by the way Christianity uses mysticism. Contemplation is something 'accessible to all Christians, who desire sincerely to do the will of God';[53] it is not just reserved for a charismatic or spiritual elite. It is also profoundly personal in its nature and impact.

Self-emptying is the key, for that is the way of Christ and of his Cross. 'In the very acknowledgement of weakness, inadequacy, and inability to pray there is a deepening longing for God. ... This hungry longing for God leads on to an experience in which the self, emptying itself of its own capacities, finds itself filled by God.'[54] Often, however, 'the light of God does blind before it can illuminate':[55] this is because of the transcendence of God, and the inadequacy of human thought and words to express His reality. It is also part of the dying to self, which is at the heart of bearing the Cross of Christ, who cried: 'My God, my God, why have you forsaken me?'[56]

The hallmark of Christian mystical experience is self-effacement, and humility is the consequence of any true vision of God in Christ. Such vision is entirely the work of divine grace; actively to seek its repetition is in vain. Instead it leads to a quiet determination to do God's will, and to be found within that will. 'Thus the contemplative finds brought into his life the unity, peace and serenity of one who is seeking God's will, one who is ready to accept whatever comes to him day by day, hour by hour, as coming from the will of God, unless it is evil or sinful.'[57] This kind of humility makes God's presence real and vivid: it is the hallmark of a saint. Many years later, in his last book, *Be Still and Know*, Bishop Michael returned to this theme:

It is by its passivity that prayer of this kind opens the way to a new pouring of the love and power of God into a soul, which is stripped naked of all but the wanting of God.[58]

* * *

In a revealing tribute to Evelyn Underhill, which he gave in 1975 to mark the centenary of her birth, Bishop Michael indicates his debt to her, as well as elucidating his own understanding of the nature of Christian mysticism still further.[59] He shows once again how influential Friedrich von Hügel was on the spiritual life of the Church of England in the years before and after the First World War, until his death in 1925. Indeed the suppression by the Vatican in 1907 of Catholic Modernism, with which von Hügel sympathized, actually had a direct and beneficial impact upon theology and spirituality in the Church of England. An example of this was the way he was able to steer the full development of Evelyn Underhill's understanding of mysticism within Christianity.

Von Hügel challenged her initial view, expressed in the first edition of her book *Mysticism*, published in 1911, that mysticism rests upon 'the supposed identity of man's soul and God', and that it is independent and even transcends the historical institution of the Church with its liturgical life and penitential discipline.[60] As a result, in the years up to her death in 1941, Evelyn Underhill 'was able to use the insights she had gained from him and from her own studies for the expression of a theology and spirituality of a distinctively Anglican kind. Few in modern times have done more to show the theological foundations of the life of prayer, and to witness to the interpenetration of prayer and theology. She has a place of her own, and it is an important one.'[61]

Bishop Michael's conclusion here is very significant, and represents his settled view on what is distinctive about Christian mystical experience: 'The Christian way, as known and expounded in the New Testament writings, is not defined in terms of mystical experience. It is a way of union with God in Christ through faith, issuing in love and hope.' Among the many gifts of the Holy Spirit along the way, he once again emphasizes 'passive contemplation', which he defines as the moment 'when the soul knows itself to be possessed by God to the depth of its existence'. He insisted, however, that 'the Christian mystic does not long for these experiences; he longs to love and serve God and to do the will of God'. In the end, 'all is God's gift, whether the mystical experience of St John of the Cross, or that kind of contemplation of God which is accessible to all those who want to want God, however feeble their wanting may be: all is of God'.[62]

* * *

The saint with whom Bishop Michael felt the closest affinity, as a scholar and Archbishop of Canterbury, was St Anselm, the second archbishop after the Norman Conquest, who died in 1109. He was an Italian, born in Aosta, who came north to the monastery of Bec in Normandy, to sit at the feet of its prior, Lanfranc. He succeeded him as prior in 1063, and in 1078 became the abbot of Bec. Much against his own inclinations, he was persuaded to become Archbishop of Canterbury in 1093 in succession to Lanfranc. His relations to the Norman kings William Rufus and Henry I were at times stormy, and he spent much of his time as archbishop in exile on the continent. He was a theologian and philosopher of outstanding stature, and also a spiritual guide and friend to many in his own monastery and further afield. This is revealed in his many letters, as well as in his more famous works, the *Proslogion*, in which he explored the nature of the existence of God, and his *Cur Deus Homo*, the most important medieval contribution to the theology of the atonement. His *Life*, written by Eadmer, one of his English monks at Canterbury, paints a vivid and attractive portrait of him, and his own prayers exerted a profound and lasting influence on later medieval spirituality. He is buried at Canterbury in a lovely chapel in the part of the cathedral that was built in his time.

Bishop Michael's hopes for rapprochement between the Anglican and Roman communions were sustained by the memory and inspiration of St Anselm. He shared this vision with Pope Paul VI, and the Pope at their historic meeting in March 1966 in Rome referred to it.[63] In April 1967 he went to visit the monastery at Bec in France to celebrate the saint's feast-day with the community there, a Benedictine monastery committed to ecumenical relationships with Anglicans. It was a memorable and happy occasion, which the Ramseys repeated privately in 1979, after his retirement as archbishop.[64] He openly said that he regarded St Anselm as the greatest of the Archbishops of Canterbury, joking with the bishops at his retirement in 1974 about a dream in which he had met several of his predecessors: 'At the end a little man came up whom I immediately recognised as Anselm. When we met we embraced each other because here I felt there was a man who was primarily a don, who tried to say his prayers and who cared nothing for the pomp and glory of his position.'[65]

The text of the address he gave at Bec in 1967 gives the best summary of what Bishop Michael valued about St Anselm.[66] Anselm came to Bec with a love of learning, but also with a desire for God. His books deal directly with the deep questions of Christian belief, without appeal to authorities apart from the Bible. They give the impression of Anselm opening his mind and soul to his readers, as indeed he did in dialogue with his pupils. There is an immediacy and intimacy to his writing reminiscent of St Augustine, who influenced him profoundly. 'One great theme was constantly in his mind, the consistency of Christian doctrine with human reason.'[67] He was led by this principle and hope, which he expressed as *fides quaerens intellectum* – 'faith seeking understanding'. This approach Bishop Michael endorsed and revered, attracted perhaps by St Anselm's independence of mind, and his fidelity to the Bible as the wellspring of the language of prayer.

St Anselm's gift for friendship attracted him also. 'We think of St Anselm as monk, priest, and pastor. Love towards God and humility in God's presence was the root of his tenderness, sympathy, and gentleness towards those in his spiritual care.' Bishop Michael loved especially the opening words of the *Proslogion*: 'Come, now, little man, put aside your business for a while; take some leisure for God: rest awhile in Him.' St Anselm could make those who met him aware of the reality of God, and this still comes across through his writings and his *Life*. 'Like a great teacher he cared for his pupils as for the truth, and the method of dialogue in his writings is a symbol of the interplay of mind with mind.'[68]

As Archbishop of Canterbury he became embroiled in political struggles in defence of the Church and of the see of Canterbury, infuriating the Norman kings by his spiritual authority, and intransigence on matters of principle. There is a splendid story in the *Life* about how his chaplain used to have to take him aside from council meetings to give him some theology to chew over; then in a better humour he could return to face the business of the day and to take decisions! 'By constancy and integrity he won battles without weapons of worldly subtlety or strength',[69] but his heart lay in his prayers, his learning and his friendships.

✳ ✳ ✳

Durham was a place close to the Ramseys' hearts, and its spiritual history meant a great deal to Bishop Michael throughout his ministry. The age of Bede, who died in the early eighth century, felt alive and near when walking with him around the cathedral and its environment. The ethos of Bede's writing appealed to him greatly, for Bede was both a historian and a theologian of the Bible, and a natural teacher. He was also a conscious disciple of St Gregory the Great, the apostle of the English and the spiritual father of medieval contemplative theology.[70] Bishop Michael commended Bede's *History of the English Church* for its humanity and candour, noting how Bede was able to make friends of his readers across the centuries.[71] He felt that the Church that Bede so lovingly described was 'our Church of England', and he was keen to alert modern English Christians to their spiritual roots and legacy.

He praised St Hilda for 'her catholicity – no faction could claim her', and for her service to early English Christian culture and education.[72] Preaching to pilgrims on Lindisfarne, he spoke eloquently of the saints whom Bede especially admired, St Aidan and St Cuthbert, the spiritual founders of Lindisfarne as a missionary and monastic centre in northern England in the seventh century. He wrote of St Cuthbert: 'He is not far from us: true he lived here very long ago, but now he lives in heaven very near to God, and prays for us, as we are praising God for him.'[73] Bede and St Cuthbert both lie buried, one at each end, in Durham cathedral.

Bishop Michael used to insist that it was vital for English Christians to know and to value their own spiritual fathers and mothers. He drew special attention to the English mystics of the fourteenth century, and their writings were ones that he revisited often during the quiet years of his retirement. He wrote about their significance and accessibility in his last book, *Be Still and Know*,[74] describing them as 'Christian writers who described in beautiful English the God-ward journey of prayer, with teaching drawn from their own deep experience'. Theirs was 'a spirituality for the people' with monastic roots anchored in the spiritual life of the hermits, at a time of great tragedy in England – the Black Death.[75]

He commended the writings of Richard Rolle who died in 1349, especially his *Fire of Love*, a work of charismatic but also contemplative spirituality. Another unknown person, the writer of *The Cloud of Unknowing*, expressed 'a deep knowledge of mystical tradition in a terse English simplicity of style'. Bishop Michael considered it to be 'as pure and classical an account of contemplation as can be found',[76] and he valued especially its descriptions of the dark night of the soul, and of the passive reception of contemplation by divine grace. 'For not what thou art, nor what thou hast been, shall God see with His merciful eyes, but what thou wouldest be.'[77]

Bishop Michael regarded *The Ladder of Perfection* by Walter Hilton, who died in 1396, as remarkable for its pastoral sensitivity and vision of the whole pattern of Christian life and prayer. 'He is very gentle: no writer expounds the approach to the night of the senses with more gentle sympathy for the frightened. But most striking is the evangelical fervour with which he tells of the person of Jesus as himself the guide and the way.'[78] Another figure of great sympathy and attractiveness was Mother Julian of Norwich, who in 1375 had some visions, which became later in her life the basis for her *Revelations of Divine Love*. Her writing showed 'what a Christian mystic can give to the world as a poet, visionary, pastor, prophet, and theologian'.[79] The crucifixion of Jesus lay at the heart of her vision of God, and in her prayers she sought for herself three wounds: 'the wound of true contrition, the wound of kind compassion, and the wound of steadfast longing towards God.'[80] She saw that it is the blood of Jesus that reveals the compassion of God for the whole creation, which is held like a tiny hazel nut in His wounded hand; and she speaks of divine motherhood as a way to understanding the tenderness of divine compassion. Faced with the implacable problem of evil, she could still humbly assert that 'All shall be well', for in the end, 'love is our Lord's meaning'.[81]

✻ ✻ ✻

As Bishop Michael moved during his retirement, he was obliged gradually to shed his great library of theological books, until at the very end there was only one small bookcase in the corner of his room in Oxford. Prominent among the few books that remained were the writings of St John of the Cross. He wrote with sure knowledge about St John and his mentor St Teresa of Avila in *Be Still and Know*.[82] They both lived in the sixteenth century in Catholic Spain; Teresa died in 1582, and St John in 1591. For them both, 'suffering proved the soil in which sanctity grew', as they struggled with the renewal of monastic and contemplative life among their Carmelite communities. The goal of their prayer was contemplation and union with God. For Teresa, action and contemplation wrestled together to the end of her life, despite her own deep experience of divine union.

St John of the Cross was plunged into the depths of suffering and contemplation as a young monk, imprisoned for a time by his own Order in Toledo. Before his escape in 1578 he had written *The Spiritual Canticle* describing his inner spiritual experience, and he followed this by a commentary on its meaning called *The Ascent of Mount Carmel*. This was followed by *The Living Flame of Love*, and in due course *The Dark Night of the Soul*, which has great similarities to *The Cloud of Unknowing*. He discounted spiritual visions, and 'wrote for those with a definite contemplative vocation'. He was self-effacing and austere in his approach: 'For while his sufferings attuned him to the way of the Cross and to the acceptance of the dark night, he was clear that the dark night is derived from the true nature of prayer itself as it approaches the contemplation of God.'[83]

Bishop Michael firmly believed that 'it matters greatly for the renewal of the Christian Church that the contemplative vocation be more known and recovered'. For 'it helps us in our feeble praying that there are those who know the dark night, and have God Himself poured into their souls'.[84] In these words he spoke from the heart of his own inner experience as someone who himself embodied the spirit of contemplative prayer. Looking back over the whole pattern of his spiritual theology it is not difficult to discern the debt he owed to St John of the Cross, even to the end of his life. These words of St John, from *The Living Flame of Love*, summarize and articulate the vision of God to which Bishop Michael consistently pointed:

> For God secretly and quietly infuses into the soul loving knowledge and wisdom without any intervention of specific acts on the soul's part, although sometimes He specifically produces them in the soul for some length of time. And the soul has then to walk with loving awareness of God, without performing specific acts, but conducting itself, as we have said, passively, and having no diligence of its own; but possessing this simple, pure and loving awareness, as one that opens his eyes with the awareness of love.[85]

Part Three:
The Church's Life

7

An Event Born in Eternity

Lord God, thou hast built in heaven and on earth a single
Church
Of truth and love and Holy Spirit;
One family and communion, whose temple is the Lamb,
One body indivisible, here and beyond:
The body of thy dear Son.
The unity of holy Church, its might, its gospel,
Proceeding from God's unalterable will,
Is truth and love and Holy Spirit.
Its ministries, O God, stream from thy heart.

*

Bishop Michael's sense of the Church's unity and reality permeates his writings, and the examination of this was one of the central themes of his first book, *The Gospel and the Catholic Church*. The rest of his life and ministry proved to be the living out of this initial vision, and the costly application of its truth to the various demands laid upon him as a Christian teacher, pastor and leader. Criticism of a church's life and shortcomings, however justified, always caused him real pain; not because he was blind to its problems, but because he always sensed that behind the institution lay the awesome mystery of the Church itself, still united to Christ's sufferings despite and through these apparent frustrations. He sought by his own sympathy and example to impart something of this vision to those who came to him for guidance, encouragement and support.

His first examination of the Church's inner life is found in chapters four and five of *The Gospel and the Catholic Church*, and many of its fundamental tenets have already underpinned earlier discussion. Because Bishop Michael stood unequivocally for the unity of the Church as Archbishop of Canterbury, and initiated so many significant dialogues with other Christian churches, it is important to establish an accurate sense of where the foundations of his own convictions lay. It has often been noted that what he wrote in his first book proved to be prophetic for the unfolding development of Anglican and other ecumenical relationships.

Bishop Michael had a complete aversion to religious individualism. The trauma of his own spiritual formation at Cuddesdon as a young Anglican ordinand made him forever conscious of the spiritual fact that outside the corporate life of the Church there is no salvation for the individual. He was wary of certain types of conversion experiences, to which individuals might cling, 'and so, in the very midst of the body of Christ, to be ensnared into an individualism and self-satisfaction which belie the truth about the one body'.[1] He came to believe that what was sometimes true of individual Christians could also prove to be true about the various Christian churches, if they clung divisively to their own traditions. The antidote lay in fidelity to Jesus as revealed in the gospels, and recognition of the pre-existence of the universal and historic Church, without which no one could be sustained in the life in Christ. In the words of St Paul: 'What do you possess that was not given to you?'[2] A Christian has to learn how to 'die to self-consciousness and self-satisfaction',[3] finding instead, 'by his place in the body, the gospel of death and resurrection active around and through him'.[4] This leads to the vital conclusion that how individual Christians relate to the Church is part of their relationship with Christ, it is not additional to it. 'Its oneness, in which they share, speaks of the truth about him.'[5] It follows then that the more deeply they enter into the reality of the Church's life in Christ, the more committed they will become to its essential unity as their consciousness of its mystery grows.

* * *

This unity springs from God Himself, expressed in the person and passion of Christ, and it is embodied also in the fundamental common structure of the Church's visible life. All who share this life constitute one race within humanity, regardless of their cultural background or denominational allegiance, and this 'one race exists first, precedes the local church and is represented by it'.[6] This reality gives to the phrase 'brothers and sisters in Christ' its unique force and meaning. What Christians have in common is their fellowship with the historical events of the gospel, wherein lie the roots of their common life in Christ; and this is set forth every time the Eucharist is celebrated. 'The unity which comes to men through the Cross is the eternal unity of God Himself, a unity of love which transcends human utterance and human understanding.'[7] To support this, Bishop Michael quoted words of Karl Barth: 'It does not mean that there is a calculable number of people who are at peace with themselves; it means that the oneness of God triumphs over the questionableness of the Church's history.'[8] The outer structure of the Church's life expresses its inner spiritual meaning and reality. The common structure of the Church is found in the gospel, in baptism and the Eucharist, and in the apostolic ministry. To achieve the recognition of this reality was the goal of St Paul's first letter to the church at Corinth: its implications were that 'the structure, historic and apostolic, does matter ... the structure of Catholicism is an utterance of the gospel'.[9]

This new race of men and women derives its unity not initially from a common belief, but from a common inner experience of Christ's redemptive act. The creeds are the expression of the belief which springs from this divine initiative, enshrined in the New Testament, and also its safeguard. To the Christians there now flow also the ancient promises of God to His people, Israel, but in a new and transformed way, which transcends racial and religious boundaries.[10] The framework within which this new way of being human exists and is extended comprises the universal pattern of 'sacraments, episcopacy, scriptures and creeds'. This raises the crucial question with which the rest of Bishop Michael's first book was concerned: 'What is the place of this structure within essential Christianity?'[11] It remained a fundamental question throughout many of his subsequent writings; and what he believed about it determined much that was most characteristic and fruitful in his own ministry as a priest and bishop.

Baptism is the common foundation of the life of the Church: 'It is a divine act which has in itself a real effect.'[12] Contrary to certain assertions about the nature of Christian conversion,

Bishop Michael said that 'baptism declares that the beginning of a person's Christianity is not what he feels and experiences, but what God in Christ has done for him'.[13] The Christian has to learn and to accept what this means, and so come to share in the family of those who in Christ experience living through dying. This is also the meaning of regularly participating in the Eucharist: for 'to understand the Bible, it is necessary to share in Christ's death and resurrection, and to be a member of his people'.[14] It is not appropriate therefore to assert the authority of the Bible over against the spiritual experience of the Church, nor vice versa. Meanwhile, the role of the creeds is to safeguard this visible structure to the Church's existence and its inherent balance, and so to provide a key to the door that leads to the life in Christ.[15]

All these four features of the Church's visible life stand together: 'The gospel has created them, and in the gospel their meaning is to be found.'[16] It is unwise to try to separate them, or to rank them in importance, and much division between Christians has arisen when any one of them has been appealed to in isolation: for 'Bible, Eucharist and apostolate are intertwined in the Lord's own utterance of the gospel on the eve of his own death'.[17] The prayer and action of Christ at the Last Supper has determined the life and shape of the Church, and the path to unity lies in recovering a proper sense of the true relationship between each of these constituent signs of the Church's life. Authentic developments within Christianity may thus be tested: do they serve the organic unity of the body in all its parts?[18]

* * *

The Church must be perceived, therefore, as a living and growing organism, whose life is partly hidden, rather than simply as an institution; for behind every individual church there stands the awesome mystery of the Church itself. No individual church can ever be defined in terms of itself, nor exist as an end in itself. Even great traditions such as Roman Catholicism, Orthodoxy or Anglicanism point beyond themselves to that perfection that lies hidden in their own partialities and imperfections. Christians must always remember that 'many fruits of the Spirit will be found apart from the full Church order',[19] and that the fulfilment of each lies in the fulfilment of all. Bishop Michael's judgement proved prescient of the vision enshrined in the statement of Vatican II, *Lumen Gentium*, about the nature of the Church. A priest is ordained, and a bishop is consecrated, therefore, to serve as a minister of the Church of God within a particular church institution. His or her ministry points beyond itself to the hidden unity and reality of the whole body of Christ, and only by the fruits of the Holy Spirit will it be known.

Bishop Michael returned to examine the inner nature of the Church in chapter seven of his book *The Resurrection of Christ*. He starts from this very important premise: 'It is in Christ, and especially in his resurrection, that the basis of the Church appears. Christians are baptised into his death and are made sharers in his resurrection.'[20] The roots of the Church's existence lie in the gospel message itself, about Jesus as the shepherd, smitten but raised up, and the temple which will be destroyed but re-founded as a living organism. 'Without the Church his mission is incomplete; but without the resurrection the Church is an idle name.'[21] The risen Christ becomes the centre of a Christian's life: he is their risen Lord with whom they come to have an unshakeable personal relationship. 'No longer do they think of Christ only in terms of his existence in history as an isolated figure: they think of him as risen and contemporary, and embracing his people as a very part of his own life. ... The Christians are his body, the sphere of the action of his risen life.'[22] This is central to the spiritual testimony of St Paul, and it is also the root of his ethical teaching.

To share in the resurrection life is therefore the hallmark of the Church's existence; but the imparting of that hallmark comes only by accepting a share in the sufferings of Christ. This is the meaning of the sign of the Cross given at baptism. The articulation of this vision of living through dying was St Paul's most important legacy to the Church's spiritual life, and Bishop Michael's words about him bear repeating:

> St Paul is ever near to the Cross in his own conflict with sin, in his bearing of the pains of others, and in his increasing knowledge of what Calvary meant and means. But in all this he is

discovering that the risen life of Jesus belongs to him, and with it great rejoicing. Awhile perhaps it may be that the Cross is more apparent in him, and the risen life may seem to be hidden. But one day the secret that is already present will be made manifest; and in the resurrection that awaits him after death he will see the risen Christ, in whose life, though hidden, he has already shared.[23]

* * *

Death and resurrection are therefore at the root of the Church's being, and this mystery is mediated through the sacraments of baptism and the Eucharist. It is appropriated through penitence and prayer, and through costly love and service of others. This hidden experience is the secret of the Church's present life, and the hope that leads it onward for the sake of human salvation. But this 'treasure is in earthen vessels; and herein lies the paradox of the Church as it is known in history'.[24] Sin too often betrays the spiritual reality of the Church, endowed as it is with the holiness of God's Spirit.

This betrayal springs from jealousy and pride, the primordial sins of mankind. Cain's cry, 'Am I my brother's keeper?', with its terrible implications, echoes from the beginning, through every page of the Bible and human history, and too often has marred the Church's ministry and witness. The crucifixion of Jesus, himself the victim of betrayal, alone can overcome this disastrous virus in human life. His self-denial and self-sacrifice, as the true shepherd and servant of God's people, is the touchstone by which any Christian witness, ministry and authority is judged, measured and authenticated. His life-giving compassion is able to save to the uttermost those who, like the criminal dying beside him, turn to him. The Church is therefore the place of turning or repentance; its worship, witness and ministry must embody this reality and make it accessible to people in their need of God.

To treat any church as an end in itself, or as an embodiment of the true Church, is therefore to misplace the kingdom of God: 'The kingdom is brought to men through the Church and is found within it: but it always transcends the Church.'[25] This was a conviction whose force Bishop Michael derived in particular from the teaching of F.D. Maurice and Charles Gore.[26] The historical reality of the Church, in all its imperfections and frustrations, is the concomitant to the reality of the incarnation and the hiddenness of God in the heart of human life. 'Men truly know the Church of heaven if they are humble enough to bear the pains and paradoxes of the visible Church upon earth.'[27] This was certainly the spirit in which Bishop Michael faced the challenges and disappointments of his own ministry as a priest and as a bishop; and he wrote these words in the midst of the Second World War:

> The Church's mission is to make Christ's passion and resurrection known, so that mankind may learn in the midst of every historical crisis both the judgement and the mercy, which the passion and resurrection bring. She fulfils her mission only by being brought herself again and again beneath that judgement and mercy which she teaches to mankind.[28]

Humility therefore befits the Church in its inner spiritual life and its outward service of others. 'From the sovereignty of Christ there flows the sovereignty of the Church which represents him. ... But this sovereignty is grounded in the Lord's humility.'[29] The title of the papacy, 'servant of the servants of God', given such weight by St Gregory the Great, defines the inner spirit of the Church and its ministry; for all are called to be the servants of the servants of Christ. From the example and action of Jesus in washing his disciples' feet at the Last Supper in St John 13, there flows the whole ministry of the Church. This title, 'servant of the servants', is the key to its most characteristic values and relationships, not least in Christian marriage, monasticism, education, and family life.[30] 'Jesus bequeaths to them a bond – this bond is the new commandment that they will love one another even as he has loved them.'[31] It is the work of the Spirit within the Church to bring this about and so to make known the riches of Christ: 'He will make them known, understood and all-powerful in human history, as the splendour of Christ is more and more reflected in the lives of men and women.'[32] This is the courageous hope, which sustains the Church's witness in the face of the tragedy and darkness that disfigure human life.

Those called to be part of the visible Church are the first-fruits of God's plan of salvation for all humanity.[33] For despite appearances, 'amid the stubborn and unbelieving world there is the Church of God. ... By the mission of the Church the judgement and the glory are made known to mankind, and the world can take its choice.'[34] This is the message of the closing discourses of St John's gospel, which Bishop Michael examined with such care and insight in *The Glory of God and the Transfiguration of Christ* and elsewhere. The same humility and loving response to God has also been at the heart of the Church's worship from the earliest time:

> Herein is the blending of action and passivity, of movement and rest, which belongs to the tradition of the worship of the Catholic Church. ... In the Eucharist the Church is united to the glory of Christ on Calvary and in heaven, and finds the focus of the glorifying of God by all created things. ... The common life of Christian fellowship is not only a witness to the glory, but is itself the glory of the Father and the Son shown forth to the world.'[35]

* * *

These therefore are the foundations of Bishop Michael's understanding of the Church, and from them he derived the guiding principles of his own pastoral and spiritual leadership as Archbishop of Canterbury. Underlying his approach lay the teaching of Charles Gore and the memory of William Temple; with them he believed that 'in the principles underlying the Anglican Communion was a microcosm of Catholic unity, scriptural and liberal'.[36] The ramifications and implications of these principles can be discerned underlying much of that he wrote at that time.

In an address early in his primacy to the World Council of Churches, meeting in New Delhi in November 1961, Bishop Michael outlined his vision of the Church's essential unity. Unity, holiness and truth stand together at the heart of the Church's life; but 'just as our mission is unity, holiness, and truth, so our scandal is the distortion of unity, holiness and truth'.[37] He derived this vision from the prayer of Jesus in St John 17: 'As the prayer is indivisible, so the fulfilment is indivisible too.'[38] Christ has already given these things to his Church: his unity with the Father, his self-consecration upon the Cross, the truth which is himself. Therefore Christian unity is not merely a human unity; it is deeper than that: 'It is for unity in truth and holiness that we work and pray.' All the many ways in which Christians already strive to do together all that they can, at every level of the Church's life and witness, speaks of 'a symphony in depth, telling of the depth of Christ's prayer and of the depth of its fulfilment'.[39]

Costly prayer and repentance is thus the inner dynamic which moves forward the recovery of Christian unity: 'Because our task is such, it has both a divine urgency and a divine patience.'[40] This patience involves patience with others, with ourselves, and with God's own 'age-long patience'. In words prophetic of his own later keen disappointment over the failure of the scheme for Anglican-Methodist reunion in 1972, he said: 'Patience includes the will to see that an apparent set-back in some scheme may be our call to go into things more deeply than before.'[41] Like Temple before him he appealed for the mutual respect of conscience between churches when differences arose, for example, over intercommunion.[42]

Theology has a most important part to play in this search for the unity, holiness and truth which sustains the Church's inner life. The diligent recovery of the common gifts of Christ to his Church becomes a 'dynamic power for the present and the future'. Bishop Michael concluded that, 'if we will be patient, true theology, good theology, is something which unites. But it will not be true unless it keeps itself and us near to the Cross whence the call to holiness comes.'[43]

One of Bishop Michael's fullest utterances about the spiritual unity of the Church is found in the first part of a book published in 1971, called *The Future of the Christian Church*, which he shared with his friend Cardinal Suenens, the Archbishop of Malines-Brussels. These lectures were given at the Episcopal Trinity Institute in New York, and it was the first time that an Anglican and a Roman Catholic primate had so collaborated.

Bishop Michael started by affirming again his simple belief that the Church 'is made by God, and given by God'. Its sacraments and ministerial order signify 'the given-ness of the Church in history, and the meaning of the Church as a sacrament of the eternal in the midst of time'.[44] As such it is never an end in itself, and this challenges all ecclesiastical structures and traditions. Instead 'it is a laying hold on the power of the resurrection. And because it is that, it is always on the converse side a death.'[45] The true quest for Christian unity disturbs human selfishness, false hopes, self-sufficiency and security; and in support of this contention, he cited words of F.D. Maurice: 'We have been dosing our people with religion, when what they want is not that but the living God.'[46] A symptom of this is the way in which academic study of theology can so easily distance people from a sense of the living God. Introducing this book, its editor quotes words of Metropolitan Anthony Bloom, which he felt described well both Ramsey and Suenens as theologians: 'Theology is knowing God, not knowing about God, much less knowing what other people know about God.'[47] Bishop Michael believed that the theologian is called to be a person of faith seeking understanding in the service of the Church's life and unity:

> The way of faith is not to try to bolster up old theology in the old ways, nor is it to abandon theology in the quest of a kind of Godless Christianity. The way of faith is rather to go into the darkness without fearing, and in the darkness to meet again the God who judges and raises the dead.[48]

The service and witness of the Church must never pander to what the world believes it wants, lest it lose its power to call men and women to repentance and forgiveness, and to an encounter with the living God. Instead religion, theology, good works all need humbling and cleansing by God's loving judgement: 'Then into the darkness the light of resurrection breaks.'[49] The result is that God becomes alive for Christians, and in them others find Him alive too. The path to this experience was blazed by St Paul in 2 Corinthians:

> Whereas 1 Corinthians gives the external picture of the Church in its glory and its shame, 2 Corinthians discloses in agony and ecstasy the inner meaning. And the inner meaning

is that, because the power whereby the Church is sustained is the resurrection, the members of the Church recapture this power only by being brought near to the Cross. When their tasks are beyond them, when they know their frailty and are ready to share Christ's sufferings, then Life is present, and Life presses on in the winning of souls and the building up of the Church in unity.[50]

Herein lies the 'essential relation of a pastor to his people, and of a people to their pastor, and of the Church to the world and the Church to its Lord'. This is the true nature of faith, to be 'near to the Cross and to the resurrection beyond it'. The impact of this is thus catholic and timeless, for the hope of the Church is 'always hope in the God of Calvary and Easter'.[51] This is not a recipe, however, for obvious peace within the Church or without it, for the challenge that it poses to Christians and non-Christians alike is very sharp, and 'if the Church bore its witness more faithfully, certain issues would be seen more sharply and simply'.[52] But by so doing, 'faith will open our eyes to the presence of God in unsuspected ways'; and 'to learn of God in new ways is not to abandon those that are old, if their claim rests not upon their being old, but upon their being timeless'.[53]

✳ ✳ ✳

Looking for what is timeless at the heart of other Christian traditions inspired and determined Bishop Michael's approach to and appreciation of English nonconformity which first nurtured him, and towards Orthodoxy to which he felt drawn and increasingly indebted.

Careful scrutiny of Chadwick's biography[54] of Bishop Michael reveals how his nonconformist inheritance under-girded his own spiritual journey and ministry. His father was a Congregational deacon in Cambridge, and a strong moral example to his son for many years. The ministers of his home church exerted a beneficial influence, and he openly avowed his debt throughout his life to Congregational theologians such as P.T. Forsyth. His conversion to Anglo-Catholicism as an undergraduate at Cambridge was a moving deeper into the mystery of Christianity rather than a complete rejection of his childhood religious formation. From his mother he inherited a lively and informed social conscience, and this protected him from the blandishments and snobbery of the Anglican establishment: his own lifestyle was always simple and self-denying. His family's Liberal political allegiance also moulded his outlook on life and social issues, and to this he clung tenaciously even when challenging the pretensions of liberal theology. He was never a reactionary. His caution towards the entanglements of ecclesiastical establishment was also etched deep by the rejection of the revised Prayer Book by the House of Commons in 1928, while he was an ordinand at Cuddesdon.[55] This caused real trauma within the church at the time, and at the very end of his primacy in 1974 he was able to secure for the Church of England its proper liberty from parliament to order its own liturgy. The nonconformist Anglo-Catholic had always refused to accept the erastian nature of the Anglican establishment in this central area of church life.

Chadwick also reveals what only his close friends knew at the time. In 1972, the General Synod finally rejected the scheme for unity between the Church of England and the Methodist church. Bishop Michael had committed much energy and hope to this project, and its loss hurt him deeply, and frustrated him in his own relationship to the church over which he presided. He regarded it as a serious Anglican betrayal of its own interests as well as those of the Methodists, a failure of vision rooted in a loss of Anglican integrity. He believed that the perpetuation of such unnecessary division impeded the work of the gospel in England. It actually shook temporarily his own allegiance to the Church of England; in sad words to a friend at Mirfield, he wrote: 'It is very painful. But I think the call is to stay, and not to despair. So we stay, and serve the Lord painfully and joyfully. What has vanished is the idea that being Anglican is something to be commended to others as a specially excellent way.' During this crisis he rediscovered in a new way the depth of his affinity with the Methodists and other nonconformists, and they saw him as their archbishop. It was during his primacy that Anglican barriers to inter-communion were removed. This verdict by his friend, the Methodist Gordon Wakefield, expressed well their esteem: 'Michael Ramsey's ecumenical theology ... could still be, if

Anglicanism remains faithful to it, the most powerful instrument for the unity of the whole people of God.'[56]

Certainly to speak to Bishop Michael was to hear the voice of an evangelical Christian, moved by that spirit of freedom and Puritan conviction that had originally given birth to the Congregational church of his childhood. He had a keen sense of personal relationship and allegiance to Christ, and of the urgency of the gospel and its demands. His approach to nonconformist and Protestant Christianity was guided also by the teaching of F.D. Maurice, a person whose own origins were Unitarian. This is very apparent in *The Gospel and the Catholic Church* where he sums up the way in which Maurice served the unity of the Church, secure in his belief that in Christ 'the divine unity has entered mankind'. This inner response to the divine gift of unity in Christ affects the quest for outer unity also: 'Unity means the dependence of all individuals, parties, movements, experiences upon the one historic family founded by Christ.'[57] To this the Protestant Reformation pointed, even if its divisive tendencies marred its witness. For 'while the assertions of the Evangelical, the Tractarian and the genuine Liberal are utterly true, the moment their assertions become "isms", falsehood ensues'.[58] Bishop Michael demonstrated by his own life and example, prayer and teaching, that it is perfectly possible as an Anglican Christian to be truly liberal, evangelical and catholic, but transcending the claims of party and of denomination. He believed that the fullness of English Christianity in all its historic manifestations was of this fundamental pattern.

Following the example of Maurice, who in his writing tried to draw out sympathetically the positive principle in each tradition of the Church, Bishop Michael was inspired to meet other people on their own ground;[59] though like Maurice he believed that partisans tend to defeat their own objects.[60] William Temple too was a guide here, for Temple believed 'that beneath every strongly held position there is some truth to be extricated and cherished. ... With unselfconscious charity, he was one with any and every group of believers in Christ in the realization of what he shared with them.'[61] Devoted as he was to Anglican Christianity, Bishop Michael never relinquished the freedom of conviction with which he had entered into its life, or the healthy detachment towards it, which his nonconformist inheritance gave him. His friendship towards Methodists and others was utterly sincere, as was his steadfast appreciation and use of the hymns of John and Charles Wesley as some of the finest expressions of English Christian spirituality.

* * *

During his lifetime as archbishop, and after his death, many Orthodox Christians regarded Bishop Michael as a figure of real spiritual authority with whom they could identify. At a formative stage in his early ministry he found a spiritual home among those Orthodox whom he met under the auspices of the Fellowship of St Alban and St Sergius. The influence upon him of Derwas Chitty and of the Russian émigrés, Zernov and Florovsky, is well discussed by Chadwick: 'He felt all the time that the centre of his own thinking was the New Testament as understood by the early Greek fathers, together with such Anglican divines as were themselves influenced by the Greek fathers. He found modern Greek and Russian religions to be in direct continuity with much of this old Greek thought.' The spirit of Orthodox worship and prayer also affected him deeply, as it had done others within the Tractarian tradition, notably Charles Gore, who in his later life had made contact with the Orthodox in Romania. At times, Bishop Michael almost felt himself 'more an Orthodox thinker than an Anglican', [62] and this is perhaps most evident in his most luminous book, *The Glory of God and the Transfiguration of Christ*.

As archbishop he was able to use this sympathy and knowledge to good effect on visits to Moscow in 1956 and 1962, and later to Bulgaria, Serbia and Romania; and by welcoming Orthodox leaders, with whom he developed a strong personal rapport, as Archbishop of Canterbury.[63] 'They saw that he understood the Orthodox religion', and it was on one of his visits abroad that he declared, 'I believe that Anglicanism has an Orthodox soul.'[64] Certainly it was unusual to have as Archbishop of Canterbury someone with so profound an affinity to a part of the Church that was still less than well known or fully understood in the West. His example did much to reinvigorate the fruitful exchange between Anglicans and Orthodox, which has always been a feature of Anglicanism since the seventeenth century. In the words of someone who knew well this side of Bishop Michael's spirituality, he was 'a man who sought to unite within himself eastern and western Christianity, and who sought to be, in some sense, Orthodox, while remaining within the Church of England'.[65]

Evidence of his early love for Orthodox worship may be detected in the way he discussed the eastern tradition of the Church in *The Gospel and the Catholic Church*. Orthodoxy he defined as 'right thought' and 'right worship', a participation in the divine 'glory'. 'For life and thought and worship are inseparable activities within the body of Christ.'[66] This vision guided his whole approach to being a Christian: 'He saw the longing for unity as an inward as well as an outward reality, an aspiration towards that reintegration of theology, prayer and life which he so constantly advocated and so remarkably embodied in himself.'[67] His experience of Orthodoxy upheld his sense of the communion of saints: 'In reverencing a saint the people reverence the life of Christ who is the life of them all.'[68] Among them, Mary is central, being closest to Jesus himself. For in eastern Christianity, 'truth is very close to life and worship. … Doctrine is always related to the body's whole life',[69] in heaven and on earth.

> The deepest initiation into eastern Orthodoxy comes not from the texts of the fathers but from sharing in the liturgy. For the worshipper will find what the textbook can never make articulate, the sense (as prominent in the east as that of the Crucifixion is prominent in the west) of the triumph of Christ who has risen from the dead, and has shattered the gates of hell; of the resurrection as the present fact about the Christians who are his body, and of the heavenly hosts whose praises are shared by the family on earth.[70]

Bishop Michael sensed that the great schism between the eastern and western Church, which became irreparable in 1054, still prevents the growth of true Christian unity: 'The schism meant, in large measure, an isolation.'[71] This became mutual with the centralizing control of the papacy and the subjugation of many Orthodox to Muslim rule by the Ottoman Empire. Although fruitful contacts continued throughout the Middle Ages, and after the Reformation also, not least between Anglicans and Orthodox, the western church has suffered an impoverishment in theology and spiritual life no less serious than the more obvious inroads endured by the Orthodox under persecution. 'Behind all subsequent schisms there stands this great schism, the parent of them all. A sundered Christendom can unite and integrate and make saints; but it can never make men whole in the inner and outer unity of the one Church.'[72] Bishop Michael's vision here anticipated that of Pope John Paul II.

Bishop Michael firmly believed that Anglican-Orthodox contact and collaboration was of service to the whole of Christendom; and he detected the hand of Providence behind the tragedy of Russian emigration in the wake of the communist revolution in 1917, by bringing riches from the eastern part of the Church for the healing of the west. The resulting sense of the centrality of the resurrection, the mystery of worship, awareness of the family of the saints and of the organic nature of the Church as the body of Christ: all these, springing from the breaking of a church through martyrdom and persecution, have 'an importance as great as that of any of the central events in Christian history. For the growing unity between east and west goes behind and brings deliverance from the failings of centuries of isolation. It does not hinder but help in healing the divisions of the west.'[73] This prophetic insight gains added force and urgency now that Communism has collapsed, and new contacts and collaboration are possible for churches east and west.

* * *

Shortly after the publication in 1936 of *The Gospel and the Catholic Church*, Bishop Michael addressed the Fellowship of St Alban and St Sergius at its summer conference in 1938. His address, published later in *Sobornost*, gives a valuable conspectus of his views, and of the spiritual principles that would guide him in later years as archbishop. He urged his hearers to attend to the inner schism within Christian life, the fragmentation of thought, worship and behaviour common to all churches and to each individual Christian. He believed that Anglican-Orthodox exchange could help illuminate and heal this interior division: 'Doctrine, worship, life utterly interpenetrate one another.' Christians are called by the Lord to an 'inward catholicity or wholeness: of the mind, the heart and the will'. Once again he appeals to the prayer of Jesus in St John 17 to demonstrate the scope of what the Spirit of God intends. For at the heart of every Christian there lies hidden through baptism the unity of Christ himself, his belief, his worship, his life: 'This orthodoxy lies deep within us all.' Its recovery is the goal of prayer and penitence, as Christian unity is forged deep within the human heart. This unity is greater than human language can fully express, though the key words of Christian theology in the Greek language of the New Testament and of the fathers have been inspired by the Holy Spirit to this spiritual end, and to enable participation in that which they describe.

This vision challenges directly each Christian who, consciously or unconsciously, perpetuates division within themselves, and between themselves and other Christians. There is a need for the healing of the rifts 'between our believing and our worshipping and our living. We all have our share in the making and in the perpetuating of these wounds. We all need the inward growth of the one new man.' Meanwhile individual churches have to accept the fragmentary and broken nature of their apprehension of the fullness of faith. 'While our grasp of life is fragmentary, our grasp of truth is fragmentary too; and authority and infallibility lie not in a dogmatic scheme but in our Lord who dwells in us and is himself the Truth.' From contact with Orthodoxy, Bishop Michael believed that 'we learn the meaning of that orthodoxy which is within ourselves, and get a vision of its fullness, and its unity of truth and worship and life'.

As the world anticipated with horror the inexorable coming of war, and the terrible confrontation with evil in the forms of Nazism and Communism, 'a theology in very close touch with worship and conflict and the Cross' was emerging within Orthodoxy, and also within German Protestantism. 'It is in the battle between the Church and Satan that theology, worship, and life are drawn together in a way that is not otherwise possible. In this conflict the Church is not only feeling the need of its outward unity, but is discovering its inward unity as well.'[74] What would emerge from such a crucible of divine remaking through the suffering lives of unknown believers in Stalin's Gulag, or through the witness of pastors like Niemoeller and Bonhoeffer in Nazi Germany?

Perhaps the words of a Russian Orthodox priest, Father Pavel Florensky, may suffice on behalf of them all: he was murdered on 8 December 1937 by the KGB in the terrible concentration camp created in the ancient monastery of Solovki on the White Sea. He wrote, 'One can give to the world only by paying for one's giving in suffering and persecution. The more selfless the giving, the severer the persecution and the harsher the suffering.'[75] This searing spiritual struggle found expression also in the vocation of another contemporary figure who died in 1938, St Silouan of Athos, who was commanded in his prayers to keep his mind in hell and never to despair. For him the sign of the Spirit's presence in a Christian, whatever their situation, was their willingness and capacity to love their enemies and persecutors.[76]

* * *

The Glory of God and the Transfiguration of Christ, first published in 1949, remains the most abiding monument to the impact that Orthodoxy made upon Bishop Michael's whole theological vision. In this book patristic teaching and deep understanding of New Testament language were inspired by a living contact with the worshipping tradition within that part of the Church which since the fifth century has always ranked the feast of the Transfiguration alongside the main feasts of our Lord.[77]

The history of the eastern theology of the Transfiguration confronts us with some of the deeper divergences between eastern and western Christianity. The east has dwelt upon the cosmic effects of the redemption wrought by Christ, and has viewed the Christian life in terms of our participation within the new creation. It is an outlook mystical rather than moral. ... The east has instinctively honoured the Transfiguration and dwelt upon its meaning with a special warmth and tenacity.[78]

In Orthodox theology, this central event in the gospels is treasured as 'a symbol of something that pervades all dogma and all worship'.[79] It provides the context in which the unity between the crucifixion and the resurrection can be seen; it is the window into the depth and consistency of the divine purpose, in the old dispensation and the new. The human witness of those called to be saints, the prophets and the apostles, points to the glory of Christ, and also to the transforming effect of participation in his death and resurrection for those who are called 'to share in the very being of God'.[80] Their communion is with him in whose image they were made and to whose likeness they are being restored. 'Nowhere is the ethos of eastern Orthodoxy far from the themes which the Transfiguration embodies.'[81] For the light shining through the face of Jesus Christ is that light, which in the beginning created all things;[82] and through the divinization of human nature the whole cosmos is being restored.[83] This call 'to see his glory',[84] the glory of the Word made flesh, follows in the way of the Cross: for 'the Transfiguration meant the taking of the whole conflict of the Lord's mission, just as it was, into the glory which gave meaning to it all'.[85]

The most considered summary of Bishop Michael's approach to and appreciation of Orthodoxy as a branch of the Church is found in the address he gave at the university of Athens in 1962. 'He who sees the Holy Orthodox Church from without feels that the ancient fathers are still alive among you.'[86] It also contains an illuminating comparison between the Anglican and Orthodox traditions, and charts the history of their contacts. He paid tribute to the way in which the Divine Liturgy 'lives and moves in heaven, where Christ is, and the Church is lifted into heaven with him. ... We see your church as the church of the resurrection, the church of the communion of saints.'[87] He asserted a common experience of Christian holy tradition, which he defined as 'the continuous stream of divine life, which is the very life of God Incarnate and of the Holy Spirit within the Church'.[88] He concluded with some perceptive comments about understanding the nature of Orthodoxy and how it is to be received, identifying as crucial 'the relation between the Church as eternal and the Church as embodied in the movement of history, and also the relation between divine Truth and the words in which divine

Truth is embodied'.[89] As a true disciple of Gore and the *Lux Mundi* tradition he declared:

> The Church of God will therefore go out both to learn and to use whatever the divine wisdom discloses in the modern world, and to meet the agonies, which are in the world. It can do this with conviction, because it knows the truth about the world and the truth about itself. The world is a place where Christ by his death and resurrection has won a cosmic victory: it is in his hands already, and all unseen his power draws it into unity. That is the orthodox faith of Christ victorious, as the fathers and the liturgy attest. The Church is a body where, amidst its many sinful and fallible members, Christ is present as the Church's inward life; and the portion of the Church on earth is ever one with the Church in paradise and heaven.[90]

✳ ✳ ✳

The secret heart of his living contact with Orthodox spirituality lay in his own personal use of the 'Jesus prayer', words which lie at the heart of eastern monastic life: 'Lord Jesus Christ, Son of the Living God: have mercy upon me, a sinner.'[91] This lovely prayer, drawn entirely from the words of those who encountered Jesus in the gospels, can become a simple focus of meditation upon the person of Jesus; or can by rhythmic prayer related to breathing become a spontaneous prayer of the heart, a loving bond of deep personal relationship with Christ. Bishop Michael once wrote: 'I think of eastern Orthodox Christians praying the prayer which came from Mount Sinai called the "Jesus prayer", drinking the name of Jesus into the soul along with the rhythms of human breath.'[92] Towards the close of his life and ministry, he commended its use in *Be Still and Know*. For him it was a key both to contemplation and to intercession:

> The repetition, many times and many times, is found to quieten the distracting parts of our personalities and to keep us wonderfully subdued and concentrated; and as we repeat the words again and again we bring into our heart the many people and needs about which we really want to pray. As the

words proceed the heart has the people on it one by one. To intercede need not mean to address phrases to God about this person or that, but to bear them upon the heart in God's presence.[93]

This brings the heart of his sanctity very close. For Bishop Michael was a person who sensed the presence of God, and communicated it to others privately, and by his preaching and leading of divine worship. He spoke of Jesus with a directness and simplicity born out of a deep love and personal knowledge of him. He saw others, near and far, in relation to Christ's burning heart of love and forgiveness, and this kindled within him great tenderness and sympathy. His road of prayer led him to fulfil the words of an unknown eastern monk: 'Put your mind into your heart, and stand in the presence of God all day long.'[94]

8

The Body and the Spirit

O Lord Jesus Christ, by thy most mighty and tender power,
Impart to me thy lowliness:
Impart to me thy purity;
Impart to me thy strength of prayer;
Impart to me thy love of the Father;
Impart to me thy perfect priesthood, and thy love of souls,
O my Lord and my God.

*

Being a Christian priest lay at the heart of Bishop Michael's life: it was its defining quality. 'Being a priest meant far more to me than being a bishop. Becoming a bishop is an incident in the life of a priest.'[1] But on both aspects of ministry he had much to teach, by word and example. He always regarded being a priest as a personal call, an act of loving obedience to the will of Christ. 'The priesthood is a divine gift to the Church: ... let there be more teaching and preaching about this divine gift of the ordained priesthood; and more prayer that love for our Lord will bring to many the faith and humility to receive his gift and his call.'[2] This ministry is sustained only by prayer, hard work and self-sacrifice: it entails a lifetime of service to others, and self-disciplined training in the arduous art of the cure of souls. It is pre-eminently a spiritual vocation: 'That is why the prayer of a priest is so supremely important, as the source of his ability to train people in the way of prayer.'[3] Whenever Bishop Michael wrote about the ministry of priests in the Church, he wrote directly from the heart of his own experience and inner conviction. Leadership in this matter was also one of the most effective aspects and abiding memories of his ministry as a bishop and archbishop.

There is a good summary of his whole approach in chapter two of *The Future of the Christian Church*. He defended the role of the ordained priests as a distinct vocation within the body of Christ: 'They are set apart for functions in a way that keeps the Church rooted in the gospel of salvation.'[4] A priest must be learned in theology and able to communicate it, not to be erudite but to be simple. It was indeed part of the genius of Bishop Michael himself that he was able to be so simple and deep at the same time, and to carry much learning lightly. This requires much hard thought and study, tested by prayer and converse with others. The teaching work of a priest should not be authoritarian, however; it prevails only through the humility of one who is willing to learn from those in his or her care. It is teaching by question and dialogue, which is the meaning of the word catechism. Central to this work of making Christ known is the ministry of reconciliation, through private counsel and confession, and in public worship. This must flow from a deep life of prayer, a conscious sensitivity to the mercy and will of Christ. 'The work of a pastor is a work of prayer, with its own intensity of sorrow and joy.'[5]

Both sorrow and joy find their focus in the celebration of the Eucharist, which gives to the gathered Church the ground of its existence, and which defines the relationship between priest and people in the one body of Christ. 'The priest is among them, completely one with them. Yet he is more than their functional representative. By his role the priest represents the dependence of the sacrament upon the historic gospel of Christ, and upon the Church as a whole in its historic continuity.'[6] In this important respect, the priest represents also the bishop. The test that confirms whether priests truly manifest Christ's authority lies in their humility, as 'slaves of Christ and servants of men and women'. In the face of a western society that finds the whole idea of a life-long commitment increasingly difficult, whether in marriage, ministry or religious profession, Bishop Michael remained convinced that it was vital to the very nature of Christianity and to the effective witness of the Church. For such self-offering mirrors, and is a response to, the self-giving of God in Jesus for the life of the world.

* * *

Communicating the gospel of Jesus is the prime duty of a priest, and central to this ministry is the art of preaching. However, 'the

Word of God is not imprisoned in the sermon; for it is present in its sovereign power even before the preacher's mouth is opened, and after the preacher's lips are closed'.[7] Bishop Michael taught that a gospel text could be perceived and handled at several levels. First there are the very words of Jesus, spoken, remembered and treasured by the earliest Christians as a means of union with him. Then there is their relationship to the whole message of Christ, their connection with the supreme moments of his life and their meaning. This in turn rests upon the way in which the apostles presented him as the crucified and risen Lord. Their goal was the same as that of the preacher today: to proclaim the presence of the one who is the Word of God. 'Those who preach the things concerning him today do so truly only if he himself is allowed to pierce through to the mind and conscience.'[8] In words that well describe what often happened when Bishop Michael himself preached, he said: 'It happens that sometimes there comes that costly simplicity whereby the person of the Lord becomes vivid, piercing to the dividing of bone and marrow.'[9] For Christ speaking through the gospel text is also Christ present in the sacrament of the Eucharist: 'The words of Jesus are spirit and life where Jesus is not merely a memory of the past, but one who is feeding our hearers with his flesh and blood.'[10]

> There is a simplicity, which is the costly outcome of the discipline of mind and heart and will. Simplicity in preaching is properly the simplicity of the knowledge of God and of human beings. To say of someone that he preaches simply is to say that he walks with God.[11]

This whole approach to preaching rests upon a pastoral and spiritual understanding of its nature, an understanding guided by a prophetic insight into the hand of God at work in contemporary events, and rooted in the profound respect for human beings which Jesus himself showed, as by word and parable he 'showed to them the meaning of themselves'. For the priest serves people in the name of God's love but also of God's truth.[12] The demands placed upon a priest, here as elsewhere in ministry, are as much in terms of what that person is called to be as to do, and that is at times very daunting. Bishop Michael addressed these words to those about to be ordained by him as Bishop of Durham:

> Often you will be knowing the joy of seeing men and women and children whose feet have been set, through your ministry, in the ways of God. But often also you will find times of frustration, baffling and mysterious; and in those times when you can see and feel no signs of usefulness or its fruits, you will know in faith, from your nearness to your Lord, that what you are and what you do are being used by him in his love and wisdom. ... As you strive to be useful you will remember the course of our Lord's mission: thirty years of hidden life, three years of public ministry, and then the waste (as it seemed) of Calvary. Useful priest, there is your exemplar![13]

There is a valuable insight into Bishop Michael's own formation as a priest in an address, which he preached at his old seminary, Cuddesdon, in 1958. Bishop Michael's homily is a personal testimony to a vision of glory glimpsed through and in the pain that he experienced during his own time there, written now in a spirit of 'gratitude searching and specific'.[14] The ideal of being a priest was transmitted by the teaching and example of mentors remembered with love. However, 'it was here that we faced the truth about ourselves before the Cross of Christ, and with the painful shattering of our pride discovered that we have no sufficiency of ourselves to think anything of ourselves'.

But by learning at the same to laugh at others and at ourselves, God is discovered as 'the author of laughter as well as tears'. The path of living through dying is joyful in sorrow and sorrowful in joy. As he said elsewhere: 'You are called by God to be someone who is sorrowful yet always rejoicing';[15] for 'our joy is the joy of those who are forgiven and forgiving'.[16] In his address at Cuddesdon, Bishop Michael drew comparison with the ascent by the disciples with Jesus of the mountain of the Transfiguration: 'The discipline was not easy for all of us. Learning to pray is difficult. Learning theology is difficult. But we were apart, and climbing, because we believed that our Lord was so leading us to give us a glimpse of his glory.' From such an encounter people then descend as those whose hearts God has touched. For them, 'the art and science of Christ and the apostles remains to learn and to practise, never to be taken as granted, always to be painfully learnt'.[17] It is learnt through prayer, and time spent apart with God.

> When our Lord went up to be transfigured, he carried with him every conflict, every burden, both of the days behind and of the days ahead. When we go apart to be with Jesus in his glory, it is so that our frustrations, our pains, and our cares may be carried into that supernatural context, which makes all the difference to them. These frustrations are not forgotten; they are not abolished; they can still be painful. But they become transfigured in the presence of Jesus, our crucified and glorious Lord. And when we have carried our frustrations up to our Lord in his glory, we find in the days that follow that he so generously brings his glory right down into the midst of our frustrations: 'My peace I give unto you.'[18]

✳ ✳ ✳

Perhaps the most treasured book that Bishop Michael ever wrote is *The Christian Priest Today*. It contains ordination charges given by him as bishop to those whom he ordained in the dioceses of Durham, York and Canterbury. It first appeared in 1972, and was significantly revised and enlarged in 1987. It remains a classic spiritual text, and for those who remember him it speaks in the way that was so inimitably his. It contains the heart of his own understanding of the priesthood, and reflects faithfully the way in which he embodied what he so deeply believed. Although these addresses were delivered over more than 20 years, strong themes run through them and reveal their inner spiritual unity.

In his introduction, Bishop Michael spoke with gratitude of the influence of the Congregational theologian, P.T. Forsyth, upon his own understanding of the Christian ministry. He quoted significant words from a book Forsyth wrote in 1917, and in a way they set the keynote for much that he himself expounded: 'In the minister's one person the human spirit speaks to God, and the Holy Spirit speaks to men. No wonder he is often rent asunder.

No wonder he snaps in such tension. It broke the heart of Christ. But it let out in the act the heart of God.'[19]

One of the strengths of Bishop Michael's writing for priests is his honest recognition of the enormous strains exerted upon those called and ordained. The hostile or indifferent attitudes in society, the frustrations within the institution of the church, anxieties over money and family needs; all these can be orchestrated by deeper and often malign spiritual pressures which sap morale and cause inner pain. It was well said by his friend and biographer, Owen Chadwick, at his memorial service in Westminster Abbey in the summer of 1988, that Bishop Michael had the gift of being able to raise the morale of clergy. This he did because he himself faced so fearlessly and openly the fact that 'no one will be nearer both to the darkness and to the light than the Christian priest today'.[20] From his own experience he knew that a person only becomes a true priest when his or her heart is broken, 'whether in penitence before the Lord or in agony for the people he is serving'.[21] Christ draws those called to his service 'to watch with him, and to watch will mean to bear and to grieve': for this opens the way into the path of the Beatitudes,[22] which is also the way of the Cross. 'The priest displays in his own person that total response to Christ to which all members of the Church are pledged.'[23]

> The door into his sorrow is also the door into his joy. As the cloud of the presence in the tabernacle was pierced from within by a burning light, so the sorrow of Jesus is the place of reconciling love pouring itself into the world, and his joy there is radiant.[24]

The priest is the ambassador of God's reconciliation in Christ:[25] he or she is called 'to bear witness to the cost of forgiveness to the divine holiness' and so become one with those who are alienated from God in their sinfulness, and alongside those who are seeking God's forgiveness in penitence and sorrow. As ambassador for Christ the priest is called to be 'one with Christ in his sorrow for sinners and in his joy at sin's conquest'.[26] This is supremely a work of prayerful love, bringing the prayer of the whole Church to bear upon the individual as they stand before God. But in the words of St Paul, 'who is sufficient for these things?'[27] The priest discovers the solemn and awesome fact that in the hands of God he or she is *nihil et omnia* – nothing yet everything. Prayer remains therefore the wellspring of effective ministry:

> It means putting yourself near God, with God, in a time of quietness every day. You put yourself with God just as you are … empty perhaps, but hungry and thirsty for him. … You can be very near to him in your naked sincerity; and He will do the rest, drawing out from you longings deeper than you knew were there, and pouring into you trust and love.[28]

As the priest elevates the chalice at the consecration of the Eucharist, he or she sees a symbol of their ministry. It is to be set apart for a unique purpose, and to be valued intrinsically as a person whose life is held firmly in God's hands. Like the chalice, the person must be stable, clean and empty, totally open towards heaven, whence the fire of God's love will descend. All that is offered has to be transformed by this fire, and then it can be offered again and again in the miracle of self-giving love, which flows from God Himself through the priest in every action of loving service and prayer for others. 'Praying with the Church across the ages and with the communion of God's saints', the priest will show the people 'that they are brought near to the awful reality of the death of the Lord on Calvary as well as to his heavenly glory'. In the pastoral ministry of a faithful priest, people will also sense that 'the Christ upon whom they feed is one with the pains of humanity around them'.[29]

Priests are called to suffer for Christ and with Christ in his mission of love and truth to the world, and to support other Christians in their own vocation with all its difficulties and challenges. It is hardly a comfortable position for anyone at times, yet how the priest handles this experience can prove life-giving for others. 'For Christians to suffer is not defeat or tragedy; it has a victorious character.'[30] God can use suffering creatively in a new work of love, and the self finds fulfilment, as it dies in order to live. This in no way diminishes the pain that is experienced; but it transforms its impact into something creative beyond itself, and often beyond our knowing. 'It is a gospel of life through death, of losing life so as to find it.'[31]

To commit oneself to this way is to be near to the secret of God's own sovereignty, near to the power which already wins victories over evil, and will ultimately prevail. That is the point at which Jesus can be shown to be near to our own world; and when he is found to be near at this point then his life and teaching are found to have their compelling fascination. ... Through his life and teaching there is the strange blending of authority and humility.[32]

* * *

The same blend of authority and humility lies at the heart of all authentic priesthood within the life of the Church. For the essence of being a priest is a hidden thing; outward action and function is but the tip of the iceberg. Solitary and unexpected can be the spiritual demands and suffering that are imposed upon those set apart to share in the redeeming work of Calvary. Self-effacement, humility and above all patience are indispensable in collaboration with God. In some ways the truest priestly witness is an angelic one, powerful by being in the background and enabling others to fulfil their vocations as Christians, a quiet but courageous ministry of affirmation and encouragement, which bears the burdens and hopes of others, their sorrows and their joys. Bishop Michael challenged his hearers to dare to be themselves as they reached out to God in prayer.[33] For only as people fully accept God's love for them can they truly begin to love others as they love themselves.

This kind of self-fulfilment in Christ lies at the basis of a catholic understanding of priestly ministry, catholic in the sense that 'if a person is to be truly converted the conversion must embrace all his personal and social relationships'.[34] For Christ calls all men and women to life in all its fullness. This has important ethical and political implications for the witness of the priest on behalf of the Church:

This is a Christian principle, the equal right of every person created in God's image to the full realisation of his powers of mind and body, and today this includes full and free citizenship with democracy as a corollary. We should, however, always distinguish carefully a non-Christian conception of the rights of people to do what they like, and a Christian concept of their right to become by God's grace their own truest selves. In this way Christianity endorses, criticises and corrects the ideal of democracy.[35]

Such a vision determines the whole pastoral strategy of the priest and the church community he or she leads and serves. It commits the priest in some situations to a prophetic witness, which will show up the corruption and impoverishment of spirit that too often grind people down. We pray in the Lord's Prayer, 'Thy kingdom come, thy will be done on earth as it is in heaven', always seeking how the divine order may be reflected in human life and society. 'Our otherworldly calling tells us of this goal, and helps us not to lose heart or lose patience, as we witness to justice, brotherhood and human dignity in the community where we are.'[36]

Amidst the vast scene of the world's problems and tragedies you may feel that your own ministry seems so small, so insignificant, so concerned with the trivial. ... But consider: the glory of Christianity is its claim that small things really matter, and the small company, the very few, the one man, the one woman, the one child are of infinite worth to God. Let that be your inspiration ... for the infinite worth of the one is the key to the Christian understanding of the many. ... You will never be nearer to Christ than in caring for the one man, the one woman, the one child.[37]

✳ ✳ ✳

No priest can give out unless he or she first takes in and goes on taking in the love and wisdom of God. Prayer and study go together, for 'faith seeks understanding', and understanding deepens love. 'Think of study as being refreshed from the deep, sparkling well of truth which is Christ himself.'[38] As St Bernard taught, the priest should be a deep reservoir from which water flows steadily, and not just a conduit or canal: it is a state of being before doing. Scripture, liturgy, the language of the creeds, the writings of the saints, all constitute this rich reservoir of experience of God and of the language of prayer. Bishop Michael said, 'I love the phrase in the Ember-tide collect – "replenish them with the truth of thy doctrine." '[39] This was his own practice, to turn to his books secretly and often, and to regard them as friends for the sake of what they contained. To explore his library was to come across many track-marks of his own attention and insight. Above all the reverence with which he used to take up his Bible spoke of his sensitivity to its unique role as the meeting-place between the mind of God and the minds of men and women.

None the less he was frank about the problems of maintaining a lively ministry over time, negotiating 'the hazards of monotony, professionalism, habit, staleness, tiredness and perfunctoriness'. He went on: 'The hard thing will be to keep alive the realisation of Christ, the lively faith in Christ to whom it all belongs. That is the great issue by which you will be judged, both as life goes on and at the final day.'[40] To this he offered three remedies: the sense of wonder in worship; the acceptance of unsought humiliations as drawing close to the suffering and the joy of Christ: 'There is nothing to fear if you are near to our Lord and in his hands';[41] and being open to Christ in other people, and to the rekindling effect of his truth and love evident in their lives: 'These Christians bring to life the faith entrusted to us.'[42] In the end, however, Christians in general, and priests in particular, 'are servants called upon to obey. Has not the idea of obedience as a Christian virtue rather slipped out of our contemporary religion?'[43]

If the will of God is that you should accept this or that interruption, and you accept them with gladness, then a day which might seem tempestuous is really filled with plan and peace and order; for where the will of God is, there is God's presence and God's peace, and where that will is obeyed there is pattern and harmony. For in His will is your peace.[44]

A priest is called to be a watchman for the coming of the Lord. How does Christ come? He comes in grief and disappointment and in the loneliness that is too often a priest's lot: 'You are near his Cross again, and you are taken out of yourself.' For 'every ordained person must come near to the grief of Jesus, seeing with his eyes, feeling with his heart'.[45] He comes in moments of blessing and success, and the sense of his joy crowns human happiness. He comes to prod his servants in times of laziness or unfaithfulness, reminding them of his judgement and the depth of his forgiveness. He comes close in times of anxiety and self-doubt: 'Whenever fretting threatens to get you down, turn to our Lord. He is grieving: think of his sorrow, and the sting of self-pity will be drawn from yours.'[46] For 'the Lord always comes to us in order to serve us; and it is for us to let him serve us. Occupied as we are in our ministry with serving him and serving people in his name, we have to face the sharpest test of our humility, which is our readiness to let him serve us.'[47] A priest who senses that Christ is at hand in this way, will inevitably make him near to others in many unexpected ways, for 'divine humility is the power which comes to make the human race different'.[48]

> By your humility you will prove that the authority entrusted to you is really Christ's. ... Let Christ be your servant. Let him serve you in the frequent cleansing of motive, ambition, and action; and then your authority, possessed in his name, will be wielded always with the humility that is his.[49]

Embracing the humility of Christ is to pass through the narrow and afflicted way that leads to life, and to that sense of heaven, which is the hidden and joyful mystery of Christianity. Of this Bishop Michael often spoke, and never more urgently than in the closing years of his life. 'Heaven is the goal of the priesthood. ... Think far more often about heaven, for there is the true perspective for our ministry from day to day.'[50] All Christians, he believed, are called to this vision, to share in a daily companionship with God, and so to enter into his joy.[51]

> To have joy in God means knowing that God is our country, our environment, the air we breathe. 'God is the country of the soul,' said St Augustine. Living in that country we do not turn away from the griefs of our present environment – indeed we may expect a greater sensitivity to these – but we are in the perspective of God, of heaven, of eternity. I believe that much of the present obsession of our church with doubts, uncertainties, nega-

tives, and loss of nerve, is due to a failure as a church to live with
God as the country of the soul. In that country we face problems
with integrity, but we also share in the joy of the saints.[52]

By his whole approach, Bishop Michael embraced those called to
share with him in the Christian ministry with great warmth and
encouragement, and this was always one of his greatest gifts, for
he was a true father-in-God. These words with which he closed
an ordination address are typical of the grace and authority he
gave away with such friendship and tenderness:

Many lives will be healed and made strong by your teaching,
your care, your love for them. ... In the coming years you will
know the wounds of Christ more than in the past, and you
will also know the peace more than you know it now. And one
day many will thank God for all that you will have done to
make the wounds and the peace known to them.[53]

✳ ✳ ✳

One of the roots of this ministry of encouragement lay in his deep
love of young people, and rapport with them, a gift he shared
with his wife, Lady Ramsey. To their regret they had no children
of their own, but their hearts were enlarged towards the many
young people who came their way. With students in particular
Bishop Michael was always most at home, fully at ease and keenly interested in their questions and opinions. He went frequently
to schools and universities as archbishop, and was always available to answer questions quite openly after lectures and services.
His acuity of mind, wit, and humility left the indelible impression
of someone who thought that being a Christian was the most
exciting challenge anyone could face. He affirmed the critical
enquiries of the young, and identified with their impatience and
their sense of justice and compassion. His sermons did much to
kindle vocation among his hearers, both because of their lucidity
and spiritual depth, and also because they demonstrated convinc-
ingly what it could mean to be a priest and servant of the gospel.
He gave to his hearers the sense that they were valued by God,
and that their vocation was to a living and loving relationship

with the person of Christ, who loved them and gave himself for them. Problems and doubts might remain, but nothing was to dim this attraction and loving obligation.

Bishop Michael retained to the end of his life a strong interest in the education of the young, and in their theological and spiritual formation in particular. He noted with concern the diminishing sense of the past and of being within a living Christian tradition of thought and prayer, and he deplored their vulnerability to the Scylla of scepticism and relativism, and the Charybdis of fundamentalism. Both approaches, he used to say, were unworthy of the Bible and its message, and tended to diminish any sense of the living God. They often stunted the development of the young person, both in mind and heart, leading to confusion, resentment against religion, and to moral laxity. In the gospels, Jesus placed the child and its needs at the heart of the kingdom of God and its values. Bishop Michael's own approach to the spiritual needs of young people is perhaps best summed up in some words of a Russian bishop of the nineteenth century, St Theophan the Recluse, who once said: 'Of all the holy vocations, the education of the young is the holiest.'

* * *

Underpinning his belief in the sacrificial vocation to the priesthood lay a profound respect and sympathy for the religious profession of monks and nuns. Bishop Michael maintained strong links with the Community of the Resurrection, founded by Charles Gore, at Mirfield in Yorkshire, with the Benedictine community at West Malling in Kent; also with the Cowley Fathers, founded by Father Benson, and with the Sisters of the Love of God in Oxford. He himself once considered a monastic vocation at Mirfield in 1936–7.[54] As Archbishop of York he did much to foster the development of a retreat house near Scarborough, which was entrusted to the sisters of the Holy Paraclete; and he became formally the Visitor of Mirfield.[55] As Archbishop of Canterbury he came to rely heavily upon the prayers of contemplative communities, regarding them as 'the praying heart of the Church'. As he travelled the world, he always appreciated the work of the more active orders in their 'caring for the distressed in Christ's name'.[56] He did what he could to encourage monastic vocations, regarding them as an important sign of the spiritual vitality of the Church.

In an address commissioning nuns to work in a parish in the diocese of Durham, Bishop Michael reminded his hearers of the key role played by monks and nuns in the conversion and formation of the English church. This could continue, he believed, in the life of the modern church, as those in religious orders brought to its activity and mission 'the hidden life of prayer' as a first priority. 'Day by day, this prayer will go on – intercession for the conversion of souls, adoration to God for God's own sake and glory.'[57] He invited the parishioners to join their own prayers to these prayers at the altar, as they shared in the prayers of the saints in heaven.

> To each of us comes the call to holiness. The particular vocation of the monk or nun to poverty, chastity, obedience, is but one form of the vocation every single Christian has at baptism: to be poor in spirit, to be pure in heart, to obey the Lord Jesus and his Church. It is terribly hard to put into words just what this holiness means. It is a matter of you and your relation to our Lord: how you are towards him in the depths of your being. And the secret is your readiness to face up to the truth about yourself before our Lord, who loves you and who died for you.[58]

In an address to the nuns at West Malling in 1966, at the consecration of their new chapel, Bishop Michael gave one of his most considered defences of monasticism. He regarded it as a specific form of Christian vocation and obedience, 'an intensely evangelical part of Christianity, rooted in the gospel story. For Jesus calls some to literal poverty, and Jesus spoke of the call to celibacy as given to those able to receive it.'[59] Bishop Michael regarded religious vows as 'the total acceptance of the call of God and a gift from God'; in that sense they mirror the vocation of the priest and are closely allied to it spiritually. In the face of a society driven by consumer greed and its attendant values, the monastic witness to the truth of God and the values of His Kingdom is never more needed as part of the Church's life. The stability of a monastery mirrors and affirms the stability of the

Christian marriage and home, and its commitment to chastity
supports the integrity of marriage and friendships, and witnesses
to the proper valuing of human sexuality in Church and society.

Bishop Michael valued particularly the *Rule of St Benedict*:
'The Benedictine way is an epitome of Christian life itself –
ideally, work and worship are utterly one.'[60] A monk or nun is
called to 'pray without ceasing',[61] and a Benedictine community
follows the principle that to work is to pray, and that to pray is
to work. This lively intercession is no flight from the world, but
an engagement with the darkness that preys upon its heart.
Elsewhere he endorsed the vision of Father Benson, who saw
Christian religious vocation as 'the contemplative gazing to God,
and doing battle with Satan, which is an essential characteristic
of all Christian life'.[62]

From monastic life, Christians can learn that they are called
not just to be people who say their prayers some of the time, but
to become people who are prayer all of the time. The separate-
ness of a monastic community undergirds the witness of the
whole Church and its mission in the darkest places of the world;
and because 'the apartness must be real and costly, the nearness
must be real and costly too'.[63] Such a community stands also for
the hidden reality of the Church's unity: its vocation is to pray
for that unity and to strengthen it in every way. 'Thus the prayer
that all may be one, by night, by day, goes on with wisdom,
knowledge, understanding, as well as with love; and this prayer
is indeed a ladder, and the top of it reaches to heaven.'[64]

> Through the centuries, Christians have found God in cloud
> and darkness, in the silence of the desert, in serving humanity,
> and all linked in the studies of the mind. We can be thankful
> that at the present time there is a renewal of the link between
> theology and spirituality.[65]

* * *

Bishop Michael's approach to being a bishop and to what that
office means in the pastoral life of the Church was governed by
his understanding of priesthood. He examined the significance of
episcopacy itself quite precisely, however, in his first book, *The*

Gospel and the Catholic Church. He established the key question early in chapter six, which deals with 'The Gospel and Episcopacy': it is 'whether this development speaks of the gospel and the one body, so that the bishop by his place in the one body bears that essential relation to the gospel which the apostles bore before him?'[66] He was concerned to ascertain the essence of episcopacy from the New Testament, and from early fathers like St Ignatius of Antioch[67] and St Cyprian, showing how the apostolic nature of episcopacy represents unity and continuity within the life of the Church.[68] 'Does this developed structure of episcopacy fulfil the same place in the Church and express the same truth as did the apostles' office ... throughout the apostolic church?'[69] His conclusion was that it did, and that here as elsewhere 'the gospel moulds the form of the Church', which demonstrates that 'Christ has come in the flesh and that his people are one family'.[70]

In the theology of St Irenaeus, 'the succession of bishops is a safeguard of continuous teaching' which is therefore apostolic in character and origin. It is also a channel of divine grace, though in no way isolated from the life of the whole Church: 'Grace is bestowed always by our Lord himself and through the action of his whole Church. Every act of grace is his act, and the act of the one body which is his.' Following the teaching of St Cyprian, Bishop Michael believed that the bishop represents this hidden ministry of divine grace flowing through the Church from age to age.[71] He quoted in an appendix some words of William Temple describing his work as a bishop in ordination and consecration: 'I act as the ministerial instrument of Christ in his body the Church. I hold it neither from the Church nor apart from the Church, but from Christ in the Church.'[72] This appears most clearly in the Anglican Ordinal – the services for the consecration of bishops and ordination of priests and deacons. Bishop Michael concluded that 'we are led to affirm that the episcopate is of the *"esse"* [or being] of the universal Church.'[73] It is therefore a deeper thing than its institutional expression in any one part of the Church, though often in history its inner essence has been obscured or temporarily lost, and sometimes even repudiated altogether.

This vision of the meaning of episcopacy governed how Bishop

Michael approached the exercise of primacy in the life of the Church. Later in the same book, he dealt with historical developments in western medieval Catholicism, criticizing the centralizing tendencies of the papacy at the expense of the local episcopate. 'It may well be argued that a primacy of a certain kind is implied from early Church history, and is ultimately necessary to Christian unity. But there is all the difference between a primacy which focuses the organic unity of all the parts of the body, and a primacy which tends to crush the effective working of the other parts.'[74] This was a classic line of Anglican objection to the manner in which the papal authority has too often been exercised, which has been a lively issue in the Catholic church since Vatican II. Its authority lies buried in the letters of St Gregory the Great, when he condemned any idea of a universal primacy as destructive of local episcopal authority.[75] But Bishop Michael's approach was never polemical, and he secured the personal friendship of Pope Paul VI, whom he deeply respected, and whose episcopal ring he treasured. He said that he was never more moved than by the sight of the Pope's pauper's coffin lying alone in the middle of the piazza in front of St Peter's in Rome.

Probably with the memory of the Malines conversations between Anglicans and Catholics in mind, Bishop Michael said in *The Gospel and the Catholic Church*, that the same test applied to the development of the papacy as applied to the emergence of episcopacy in relation to the gospel and the Church's inner spiritual unity: 'A papacy, which expresses the general mind of the Church in doctrine, and which focuses the organic unity of all the bishops and of the whole Church, might well claim to be a legitimate development in and through the gospel.'[76] But if it overrode the *sensus fidelium* (the common mind of the faithful) and the free functioning of bishops, it erred. Only as these were renewed spiritually would the true meaning of such a primacy become clear.[77] In this his early teaching he anticipated the later deliberations of ARCIC – the commission which he and Pope Paul set up to resolve the historic differences between Catholics and Anglicans.[78]

* * *

Bishop Michael's own approach to the exercise of primacy within the Church of England and the Anglican Communion was guided consciously by the teaching and example of St Gregory the Great about being the servant of the servants of Christ. He read St Gregory's *Pastoral Rule* on the eve of his own consecration as a bishop, and he often paid tribute to him in his preaching and writing. In his mind, Anglican bishops and archbishops are called 'to be servants of the gospel of God and of the universal Church'.[79] He quoted with approval some words of F.D. Maurice: 'I have always loved episcopacy as expressing the fatherly and catholic character of the Church',[80] and certainly Bishop Michael was himself that kind of bishop.

What he appreciated most in those bishops who had gone before him comes out occasionally in his preaching. At his enthronement in Durham Cathedral in 1952 he spoke warmly of his beloved predecessor, the great New Testament scholar Westcott, a person who combined the love of learning with statesmanship and 'an otherworldliness which lives in touch with things unseen'.[81] He was a bishop whose Christianity was 'marked by a passion for truth, a concern for man's common life, and a hunger for another world'. He also extolled John Cosin, another predecessor at Durham of the Restoration period, as a father of *The Book of Common Prayer*, and as someone whose 'name lives to remind us that even in days most dark and difficult God reigns and can restore and recreate'.[82]

In a sermon preached in 1962 at the installation of a new bishop of Washington in America, Bishop Michael described a bishop as a 'shepherd, teacher and intercessor' following the example of Jesus himself. The bishop embodies the call of God to His people to become saints: his office points beyond itself in the direction of the heavenly fulfilment of all the Church's life and witness.[83] In his own enthronement address in Canterbury Cathedral in 1961, he had addressed the same themes, adding that the bishop is not alone: 'There goes with him the great band of those whose hearts God has touched with the faith of Christ.'[84] Preaching ten years later in 1971 to mark the centenary of the birth of the great Anglo-Catholic missionary bishop Frank Weston, Bishop Michael quoted words Weston had spoken in 1923:

You cannot claim to worship Jesus in church unless you pity Jesus in the slum. Go out into the highways and hedges, where not even the bishops will try to hinder you! Go out and look for Jesus in the ragged and the naked, the oppressed and the sweated labourer. Look for Jesus, and when you see him gird yourselves with his towel and wash his feet.[85]

Bishop Michael devoted a closing chapter of *The Christian Priest Today* to the work of a bishop. He again commended St Gregory the Great's *Pastoral Rule* and said that 'the bishop is still a priest, and unless he retains the heart and mind of a priest he will be a bad bishop'.[86] By his ministry of prayer, he will become 'the priests' priest and the people's priest', a person whose humanity and breadth of vision and interest 'will represent both the Church's apartness, and its identification with the wide concerns of the community'. Only his humility will vouch for the heavenly source of his authority, but that authority will commend itself by a willingness to learn and to listen as well as to speak with conviction. 'As the keeper of the tradition of Christ he will know what are the things which are not shaken.'[87]

A bishop's ministry will not be immune from sorrow and disappointment: 'It may be the will of God that our church should have its heart broken, and if that were to happen it would not mean that we were heading for the world's misery but quite likely pointing the way to the deepest joy.'[88] Jesus said to his followers: 'You are salt to the world. But if salt becomes tasteless, how is its saltiness to be restored?'[89] He answered his own question by the blood, sweat and tears of Calvary: only from his broken heart flows out the living, life-giving water. It flows into the life of both Church and society only through lives joined in sometimes painful union with him, who is the head of the Church which is his body. Episcopacy and priesthood are at times akin to martyrdom; and to each priest and bishop are directed the prophetic words that Christ spoke to St Peter: 'In truth I tell you: when you were young you fastened your belt about you and walked where you chose; but when you are old you will stretch out your arms, and a stranger will bind you fast, and carry you where you have no wish to go.'[90]

This lovely prayer comes for a staff along the way from the

heart of Bishop Michael's own experience as a priest and bishop, and it speaks directly to all those called to follow his footsteps in the Christian ministry:

> Lord, take my heart and break it: break it not in the way I would like, but in the way you know to be best. And because it is you who break it, I will not be afraid, for in your hands all is safe and I am safe.
>
> Lord, take my heart and give to it your joy, not in the ways I like, but in the ways you know are best, that your joy may be fulfilled in me. So, dear Lord, I am ready to be your deacon, ready to be your priest.[91]

9

Anglican Catholicism

Grant us, O Lord God, to approach Thine altar,
With the whole fellowship of Thy redeemed.
Grant us to do Thee honour and worship,
With exceeding humility and suppliant reverence,
With holy intention, and a faith full and aflame.
Grant us to seek and to abide in Christ,
In his truth, his love, his life;
For these are eternal and are all himself,
Who lives and reigns with Thee and the Holy Spirit,
One God, now and for ever.

*

'The Church of England is part of the one, holy, catholic and apostolic Church, worshipping the one true God, Father, Son, and Holy Spirit. It professes the faith uniquely set forth in the catholic creeds, which faith the Church is called upon to proclaim afresh in each generation. Led by the Holy Spirit, it has borne witness to Christian truth in its historic formularies, the Thirty-nine Articles of Religion, the *Book of Common Prayer*, and the Ordering of bishops, priests and deacons.'[1] These moving words open the Declaration of Assent, which all those ordained to serve in the Church of England must make. They constitute the most succinct yet adequate statement of the Anglican understanding of its own form and tradition of Catholic Christianity.

It was Bishop Michael's firm conviction that the roots of the Anglican Church lay deeper than the events of the Reformation, even though these were determining of its present shape and character. His own affinity with the vision of St Gregory the Great, the humane wisdom of Bede, the clarity of thought and prayer enshrined in the writings of St Anselm, and the profound simplicity of the medieval English mystics, anchored him in a living tradition stretching back over 1400 years. He once said that becoming Archbishop of Canterbury intensified this sensitivity for him, and sustained his ministry in that difficult office. He believed that it was vital for English-speaking Christians to sense and to know this stream of spiritual experience, and to allow it to influence and support the witness of the Church today.

It can be argued that one of the main factors, which determined the *via media* of the Church of England between Catholicism and Protestantism in the sixteenth and seventeenth centuries, was the reality of the *Ecclesia Anglicana* already long established during the preceding thousand years of the Middle Ages. The relative political isolation of England, especially during the Anglo-Saxon centuries, meant that the spirit and teaching of St Gregory the Great, popularized by the biblical and historical writings of Bede, took deep root and determined the essential character of English Christianity. This came about in large measure because of the widespread influence of Benedictine monasticism before and after the Norman Conquest. These roots ran deep into the spirit of English prayer, because from the beginning Christianity was bi-lingual, expressing itself in English as well as in Latin. From the prayers of the Anglo-Saxons, through the writings of the medieval mystics, to the genesis of *The Book of Common Prayer*, a common tradition and spiritual vision can be perceived.

The position of the Archbishop of Canterbury also gave to the English church a sense of unity, history and mission, and the influence of its incumbents could sometimes stretch into the life of the continental church as well, as English missions went to Germany and Scandinavia during Anglo-Saxon times. Later the particular antiquity of the link with Rome meant that the Archbishop of Canterbury was regarded there and elsewhere as the 'pope of the other world' – across the Alps. Another line of distinctive continuity lay in the close link between the Church and the Crown, established during Anglo-Saxon times, and going back to the very beginnings of the Roman mission. As a result law, justice and the administration of the Church were inextricably entwined in the structure of the medieval state, limiting the power and influence of the Crown and also of the papacy.

From at least the time of St Dunstan, when an Archbishop of Canterbury came to crown an English monarch, he called him or her to account as shepherd and servant of God's people, and extracted a solemn promise to maintain justice and the freedom of the Church, and to rule under law, as the precondition for the Church's anointing and blessing. The corollary to this tradition was an innate rejection of prelacy, the exalting of the power of churchmen in the life of the state: from Wilfrid and Becket to Wolsey and Laud a tradition of repudiation of over-mighty bishops can be discerned, which preserved the English Church to some extent from many of the worst excesses of the later medieval and renaissance Church in Europe.

When the Reformation occurred in England, despite the murky political circumstances that were its catalyst, a national church emerged which could claim to be the heir and successor to the medieval church, while embracing some of the most important teaching of the Protestant reformers. The retaining of the historical episcopate and the link with the Crown symbolized this deeper spiritual continuity, which found expression in *The Book of Common Prayer* and in the language of the *Authorized Version* of the Bible. The roots of this beautiful expression of Christianity lay in the later medieval piety associated with Langland's poetry, the writings of Margery Kempe, and the devotional literature of the fifteenth century, which mirrored the extensive rebuilding at that time creating so many lovely parish churches throughout the land. Perhaps the most attractive picture of this pastoral spirituality, sometimes associated with Wycliffe and his Lollard followers, is painted by Chaucer in his sketch of the poor parson, who was 'rich in holy thought and deed', a devout preacher, teacher and shepherd to his people, who first acted and then taught, mindful as he said 'that if gold rust, what shall iron do?'[2]

It was upon this deep foundation that the theologians of the Anglican Church after the Reformation came to build its defence and spiritual teaching. Bishop Michael used to point out that the first Archbishop of Canterbury appointed by Elizabeth I, Matthew Parker, collected with great energy manuscripts from the Anglo-

Saxon church, now in the library of his old college, Corpus Christi College, Cambridge, in order 'to show that a number of features of the Elizabethan church were not new inventions, but familiar to the Catholic church in England in its earlier centuries', and that at the heart of its life, 'its gospel, its creeds, its sacraments, its ministry and a good deal of its customs – it was essentially the same church'.[3] In a collection of lectures, delivered at Nashotah House, an Episcopal seminary in America that he loved to visit during his retirement, he went on to extol the thought and work of Richard Hooker, the foremost apologist of the Anglican Church during the sixteenth century, who died in 1600.

* * *

Bishop Michael portrayed Hooker as a faithful and intelligent parish priest, and discussed his concept of tradition within Anglicanism: 'The close connection between theology, doctrine and Christian worship is very powerful in Hooker.'[4] Hooker's confidence in the spiritual authority underlying this tradition was balanced by a suspicion of any claim to infallibility within the life of the Church. Belief in revelation by God did not commit anyone to 'claims for the infallibility of the language in which God's revelation is at any time expressed'. Hooker felt keenly the sense of mystery that surrounds every communication by God of Himself to human beings, and Bishop Michael quoted Hooker's famous statement about the reality of the mystery of Christ's presence at the moment of communion in the Eucharist: 'Why should any cogitation possess the mind of a faithful communicant but this, "O my God thou art true, O my soul thou art happy!"'[5] Bishop Michael also drew attention to Hooker's insistence that God's revelation is implicit within His creation. Divine reason operates everywhere and always, in many hidden ways; and human reason and conscience respond to His presence and His call. 'For what God does in revelation brings to a climax what He does in nature, and what He does in nature is a necessary key to the understanding of what he does in revelation.'[6]

Hooker was heir to the thought of the Renaissance as well as to the English Christian tradition, and the approach he took gave to the doctrine of the incarnation a centrality in classical

Anglican theology that it has never lost. Part of this approach expressed itself also in discriminating between those doctrines of Christianity that are necessary to salvation and that have their roots in the Bible, and those 'things indifferent' – in Greek *adiaphora* – upon which Christians may differ, and do differ. 'Scripture tells us what is necessary for salvation, but it is not a source of authority for countless other things as well.'[7] This is also the position taken in the *Thirty-Nine Articles* that were appended to *The Book of Common Prayer*. It remained fundamental to the whole defence of the Anglican Church, which preoccupied its theologians in their dialogue and controversies with Roman Catholicism on the one hand, and Protestantism abroad and Puritanism at home on the other.

It is interesting to compare Bishop Michael's teaching at this closing stage of his active ministry with what he wrote as a young theologian in his first book, *The Gospel and the Catholic Church*. In chapter thirteen of that book he talked about the 'Ecclesia Anglicana': he was concerned to show how 'this Church of England cannot be explained in terms of politics alone'.[8] For although the most striking result of the Reformation was to put the Bible in their own language into the hands of ordinary people, Anglican theologians immediately and consistently interpreted it within the context of 'the primitive church with its structure and tradition'. He quoted a representative Anglican opinion of the early seventeenth century, which described 'the true Church of God in the primitive ages' as the 'canal or conduit pipe to derive and convey to succeeding generations the celestial water contained in Holy Scripture'.[9] The Bible indeed contains the Word of God, but in the sense that, for Christians, it 'centres simply on the fact of Christ himself', and he is intelligible only within the continuing life and worship of the Church. This appeal to history was symbolized for early Anglicans in the continuing existence of episcopacy: 'For its existence declared the truth that the Church in England was not a new foundation, nor just a local realisation of the invisible Church, but the expression on English soil of the one historical and continuous visible Church of God.'[10]

* * *

Those who followed Hooker, sometimes called the Caroline divines, 'appealed to the Bible as the test of doctrine, and also to the Fathers and to the continuous tradition of Church life, both in the west and east alike. Their study of Greek theology gave to the churchmanship of these seventeenth-century divines a breadth which reached beyond the west and its controversies; their idea of the Church is summed up by Bishop Lancelot Andrewes when, in his *Preces Privatae*, he prays "for the whole Church Catholic, eastern, western, our own." '[11] By a happy chance one of the last books for which Bishop Michael wrote a foreword was a major study of Lancelot Andrewes' preaching.[12] He hailed him as 'a divine of outstanding depth and spirituality who brings inspiration to our contemporary spiritual strivings'. He commended the way in which Andrewes went behind the controversies of the day and dug down to the roots of the Church's life. He commended also the way in which he united theology and prayer. Andrewes related deeply and directly to the fathers as a living symphony of testimony to the reality of God's love and truth, revealed in Jesus to every age of the Church's history, and made real by the Holy Spirit.

Lancelot Andrewes, who died in 1626, repays close scrutiny as a bishop of kindred spirit to Bishop Michael, who surely exerted a hidden influence on his own spirituality, and on the way in which theology and prayer became so deeply united within him, that for many in his generation Bishop Michael embodied the spiritual genius of Anglicanism. Andrewes became Dean of Westminster when James I came to the throne in 1601, and in time held in succession the sees of Chichester, Ely and Winchester. He was an outstanding preacher, highly regarded by the king and his court, and his sermons reflect the depth and breadth of his scholarship, and also of his prayers. His book of private devotions, the *Preces Privatae*, has always been treasured as a classic expression of Anglican spirituality.

Andrewes was described at his funeral as a person whose life was a life of prayer; he was also a diligent scholar who would brook no interruption before midday. Brightman, the Tractarian editor of the *Preces Privatae*, portrays his learning as 'scholarly, historical, and inductive, rather than speculative and creative'.[13] As a bishop he did not hesitate to make stern moral demands upon his colleagues, calling for holiness and learning among the clergy and in the wider life of the Church. He lamented the loss of a sense of worship: 'Now adoration is laid aside, and with the most, neglected quite. Most come and go without it, nay they scarce know what it is.'[14] But demanding as he was upon himself, he did not impose his own style of worship upon others; 'he was content with the enjoying without the enjoining.'[15] He was widely regarded as a saint in his own lifetime, a man of a 'whiteness of soul' that was respected by all who knew him. The basic axiom of his life was not unlike that of St Anselm: 'Without knowledge the soul itself is not good'; and he deeply opposed what he described as 'ignorant devotion, implicit faith and blind obedience'.[16] His kindness and generosity were legendary, and his commitment to peace within the life of the Church was never in doubt. 'In an age of new ecclesiastical systems, he was content and more than content with the traditional system as he found it represented in the English Church, in so far as that was true to itself.'[17]

His sermons sprang out of his prayers and were sustained by them,[18] and the author of the most recent study of them draws some important conclusions as to their spiritual significance.[19] The centrality of the incarnation governed the whole way in which Andrewes tried to communicate the reality of the person of Christ and the possibility of relationship with him. Its paradoxical character reflects the mystery of God's self-giving, and has important bearing upon every area of human life and worship. The clarity and precision of his thought, and his fidelity to the classical Christian definitions of Christology, were means to a single end, 'that of pointing to the way of salvation in Christ'. Both Hooker and Andrewes 'called the attention of their contemporaries to the quite central character of the reality of God made man'.[20] By becoming a Christian, a person enters into a life-giving union with God in Christ. 'Everything begins and everything ends in Him. ... There is no province of life that may not be illuminated by his divine-human person: the Church, the sacraments, public life, private life, and the whole creation.'[21]

This life-giving union or deification is the work of the Holy Spirit in collaboration with the human will. His emphasis on the work of the Holy Spirit 'is without doubt the most distinctive characteristic of the theology of Lancelot Andrewes'.[22] The experience of communion with Christ in the Holy Spirit is shared with all Christians; it is never merely an individual phenomenon. This common experience of life in the Spirit is expressed in the Church's tradition, which thereby safeguards the possibility of entering into this spiritual reality in any age of history. The Eucharist is the summit of all sacramental life: it is 'the highest form of union with God here below'.[23] Like Hooker, Andrewes insisted on what is at the heart of the Eucharist – the reality of communion with Christ, crucified and risen. Fundamental to his sacramental theology was the Greek term *anamnesis* – or 'memory': in the Eucharist Christians participate in the living memory of the Church, which is the same across the ages, because Jesus Christ is known, loved and adored as the same person, yesterday, today and for ever.

This is the apostolic faith, expressed by those who in every generation have become fathers and mothers of the Church's inner life, true witnesses to Christ as the way, the truth and the life. Theology is therefore 'progression in the experience of the mystery' of life in Christ, and it exists 'for the service of the entire man on his way towards union with the personal God, the way of deification'.[24] The goal of this way is that fullness of a truly catholic faith, which lies at the heart of the Church's hidden unity; for fullness comes only when a person is united to God. This saying of Evagrius of Pontus aptly describes Lancelot Andrewes, as indeed it does Bishop Michael too: 'If you are a theologian, you pray truly; and if you pray truly, you are a theologian.'[25]

* * *

The Tractarian reformers in the middle of the nineteenth century found in Lancelot Andrewes a seminal influence, and were responsible for editing his theological writings and promoting the *Preces Privatae*.[26] One of those who especially appreciated Andrewes was Dean Church. Bishop Michael discussed Church's verdict on Andrewes in a review he wrote in 1958 of a new study of Church's life. Church had said, in an essay on Andrewes, that the formation of the Church of England began in the reign of Elizabeth I, but its completion only occurred in the later seventeenth century, especially in the years after 1662. In Bishop Michael's words: 'There was a century of adjustment by divines who worked out the appeal to antiquity with a fullness and balance not always attained by those who first proclaimed the necessity of that appeal.'[27]

Dean Church published in 1891 the finest account of the Tractarian or Oxford Movement, and his evaluation of its origins, vision and development, in which he had been an active participant and close friend of Newman, clearly appealed strongly to Bishop Michael, who regarded Church as 'one of the greatest Anglicans'.[28] Bishop Michael was himself heir to the spiritual legacy of the Tractarians, and he praised Church for his 'cool judgement brought by a sense of history, and the conviction that civilization and culture have a positive meaning for the Christian'. He contrasted this sharply with Newman's weaknesses in these areas, observing that 'the disciple had what the master had lacked'.

Bishop Michael also noted Church's role as Dean of St Paul's Cathedral in London, presiding over a remarkably gifted and influential chapter of clergy that included Lightfoot, Liddon, Stubbs, and Scott Holland. His Anglicanism was 'the conviction of a quiet and sober faith', and like John Keble, the prime mover of the Tractarians, whose portrait he had painted with such care and sympathy in his history, Church 'saw in the Oxford Movement the gateway to a view of the Anglican vocation that was larger and less cramped than the interpretations which had previously prevailed'. To him 'catholicity and liberality went closely together', as his sensitive studies of Dante and St Anselm reflected. His was a theological approach rooted in historical study, which was Cross-centred, perceptive of divine providence, and open to the sense of heaven. These were all qualities to which Bishop Michael warmed, and in private conversation he often directed attention back to this original vision of the Tractarians.

Bishop Michael esteemed Keble in particular as a person who made God real to others, once quoting from a letter that described how a person in some spiritual confusion 'lived with John Keble for a month or two. John Keble said no word of controversy, but simply lived. And my friend's faith was restored and his place in the Anglican Church was restored.'[29] Recalling one of Newman's great sermons about the spiritual nature of the Church, Bishop Michael articulated towards the end of his life his own appreciation of the Tractarian vision:

> On that Mountain of the Lord, you see, are the saints of every age. The Church can be described both as an historical institution, with a pedigree from the past, and also as the contemporary supernatural action of the living Christ through the sacraments, the Word, and the existence of the people of God on earth.[30]

❋ ❋ ❋

Chadwick in his biography charts quite precisely the influences that brought Bishop Michael into the orbit of Anglo-Catholic worship and thought. It was in the church of St Giles, opposite Magdalene College where he was an undergraduate, that he first entered into the 'mystery and awe' of the Catholic tradition.[31] Its spiritual depth was mediated to him by a number of sympathetic and influential priests in Cambridge at that time, who belonged to a group called the Oratory of the Good Shepherd. Bishop Michael remembered one of them with special affection, and his photograph always hung prominently in his study: this was Eric Milner-White, later Dean of York, whose prayers preface the chapters of this book. He said of Bishop Michael's appointment in 1956 to work with him as Archbishop of York: 'My child in the Spirit has become my father-in-God.'[32] This spiritual nurture and encouragement was matched by the intellectual impact of the leading Anglo-Catholic scholar of the New Testament, Sir Edwyn Hoskyns, then Dean of Corpus Christi College.[33]

When Bishop Michael moved from Cambridge to Cuddesdon to train to be a priest, he encountered another facet of the Tractarian legacy. Bishop Samuel Wilberforce of Oxford had founded the college at Cuddesdon in 1854 to train clergy, and its ethos was Tractarian through and through.[34] Its aim was to complement the traditional study of theology at university with a disciplined formation in the spiritual life of prayer, in preparation for pastoral ministry. One of the most formative influences in the college's development was Edward King, who went there as chaplain in 1858. After a serious crisis of confidence in the leadership of the college in 1859, he was eventually appointed its principal in 1863. As principal he was also parish priest of the village, so the spirit of prayer in which clergy were formed at Cuddesdon was rooted in the pastoral ministry of a normal church. King's leadership left a permanent mark on the spiritual ethos of Cuddesdon: 'His teaching married heart and head, devotion and dogma, in a quite inimitable manner.'[35] His portrait in the refectory captured his glance, sensitive, kind but searching. In 1873, King returned to the university in Oxford as professor of pastoral theology at Christ Church. Looking back in 1900, he spoke warmly of his love for Cuddesdon as a hill of vision, and a place where God became real: 'It was here that I learned to realise more than I ever did before the possibility of the reality of the love of God and the love of man. ... My life here gave me hope of a higher life for myself, and a higher life for other people too.'[36]

In Oxford his remarkable spiritual ministry continued, as did his friendship with Father Benson, and he exerted a wide influence upon the religious life of the university and upon many who later became leading scholars and churchmen. His teaching and capacity for pastoral relationships were described as 'so human, so sagacious, so penetrating, and so devout'.[37] More hidden was his work as a confessor and spiritual director, where his holiness and gifts of friendship made him a potent ambassador of Christ.

In 1885, he was appointed by Gladstone to serve as bishop of Lincoln, where he proved the first great Tractarian bishop of the Church of England. These words of his friend, Scott Holland, proved indeed prophetic: 'It shall be a bishopric of love – the love of God behind, and above, and about you! The love of the blessed Spirit, alive with good cheer within you! The love of the poor shining out from you, until they kneel under its lovely benediction.'[38] The full story of his episcopate is told elsewhere,[39] but in his own lifetime he was regarded as a saint; he died in 1910, and his memory proved enduring and highly influential. In the words of Archbishop Cosmo Lang: 'He was the most saintly of men, and the most human of saints.'[40] His own favourite text from the Bible were the words, 'Thy gentleness hath made me great'.[41]

* * *

The other figure that was part of the living spiritual past at Cuddesdon was Charles Gore, to whom reference has often been made throughout this study. Bishop Michael remembered his preaching with vivid appreciation, and always spoke about him with great warmth and reverence for his intellectual and spiritual leadership. He once said that 'Gore's influence on him had been profound, and that whatever degree of coherence he had in theology, he owed to Gore'. He believed this was also true for William Temple. [42] Towards the very end of his life, he used to urge a return to the thought of Gore, still believing that it held the key to Anglican integrity and identity in its evangelism, prayer and social witness.

Gore was a friend and protégé of King's, and in 1880 became vice-principal of Cuddesdon, before becoming principal of Pusey House in Oxford in 1884. With the departure of King to Lincoln the next year, Gore became the leader of the heirs of the Tractarians, and exerted great spiritual and moral influence in Oxford and beyond. In 1889, he edited and contributed to the famous volume of essays called *Lux Mundi*, which, to the discomfort of some, admitted the role of biblical criticism and scientific enquiry in relation to theology. He was also instrumental in creating the Christian Social Union to address social problems and injustices; and in 1893, he and a group of friends founded the Community of the Resurrection, which later settled at Mirfield in Yorkshire. From 1894 he conducted an influential preaching ministry in London as a canon of Westminster Abbey, and in 1902 he became bishop of Worcester, using his position there to help create the new see of Birmingham, which he served as its first bishop. In 1911 he was moved to be Bishop of Oxford, but in 1919 he resigned in order to devote his energies to an extensive programme of theological writing, the most notable of which was *The Reconstruction of Christian Belief*. He was also active in ecumenical contacts with both Catholics and Orthodox, and died in 1932. In his day and for long afterwards, he exerted a commanding influence upon the Church of England and its theology.

The theology of Bishop Michael was built upon the teaching and example of Charles Gore, in both its biblical, social and spiritual aspects. In many ways the secret of his life and ministry was that he faithfully lived out what Gore had taught, embodying in his own person, and by his inner prayer and suffering, its costly but life-giving message. He examined Gore's teaching in a lecture given at Westminster Abbey in 1954 entitled *Charles Gore and Anglican Theology*, and later in much more detail in his major study *From Gore to Temple*, published in 1960. This book deals with many aspects of Anglican theology in the first half of the twentieth century, but underpinning his treatment of Gore is a perceptive and profound understanding of the spirit and significance of his prophetic ministry, example and teaching.

Central to Gore's thought was the historical reality of the incarnation, and it was part of his achievement and legacy that this doctrine remained central to Anglican theology for many years to come. *Lux Mundi* was a turning point from which there was no going back. Its writers, led by Gore, focused on the incarnation as the key to understanding all human experience and knowledge, confident that if the Creator had entered history as the re-creator of fallen humanity, then all truth, however perceived, points to Him. 'Either God is everywhere present in nature, or He is nowhere. He cannot be here and not there.'[43] It was Gore's achievement to ensure that this positive vision did not lapse into a vague benign belief in the inevitable immanence of God in nature and human life. Bishop Michael's verdict on his handling of this issue, about which there was much debate at the turn of the century, remains of crucial importance for Anglican theology:

> The difference between Incarnation and immanentism is absolute. Though God is significantly manifested in the created world, and though there is the affinity between God and man implied in the creation of man in the divine image, nonetheless the most saintly men and women are not in virtue of their saintliness divine, and the creature is not the Creator. It is this which has been for Anglican divinity the supreme significance of the doctrine of the two natures in Christ. This doctrine attests the paradox of the incarnation, whereby one who is divine and the Creator humbled Himself to take upon Him the creaturely life of man.[44]

History therefore assumes a key role as handmaid to Christian theology, as it did for Richard Hooker and Lancelot Andrewes long before. Gore was steeped in a historical approach to the Bible, and read widely in the writings of the fathers. Throughout his life until its end he used to assert that the historical basis for Christianity was secure and can be known by sound historical research. His view was that 'patient and prayerful enquiry can establish, not absolutely but adequately, the mind of the Catholic Church'.[45] As Gore himself once put it, 'the inward assurance (of Christian faith) is made to rest upon facts',[46] because it is about relating to an actual divine person. Christ may have expressed and crowned the outcome of long centuries of human history and development, but essentially his incarnation was 'the unique act of God, doing what could only be done once and for all'.[47] This was the supreme miracle at the heart of Christianity, and the historical evidence of the gospels could only be set aside if prejudice dictated the impossibility of miracle. Gore himself knew keenly the pain of the world, but hoped deeply in the love of God breaking in to make all things new. 'Miracle was to him the vindication of the living God intervening to restore a created world wrecked and disordered by sin',[48] even if the full pattern of that divine intervention often remains painfully obscure.

* * *

The humility of God revealed in the coming of Jesus, and the cost of divine love revealed upon the Cross were expressed by Gore and by those who followed him in the doctrine of *kenosis* – the self-emptying of God in the person of Christ. Bishop Michael explored this central conviction with great care in chapter three of *From Gore to Temple*. Christ 'emptied himself, as one pouring himself out':[49] *kenosis* therefore expresses a dynamic mystery of self-giving and relationship, rather than describing a static or ontological state of being. The language of St Paul in Philippians 2:5f and also in 2 Corinthians 8:9 pointed the way, but it was by no means a new doctrinal emphasis in the history of the Church.

Gore was concerned to do full justice to the humanity of Jesus as recorded historically in the gospels, fully aware, however, of the limitations of knowledge about the inner psychology of Jesus in his relationship to God, and aware too of the difficult questions raised by this theory about how Jesus could truly be both

God and man in one person. In his Bampton lectures of 1891, published as *The Incarnation of the Son of God*, Gore asserted that 'the method of God in history, like the method of God in nature, is to an astonishing degree self-restraining ... it is the higher power of love which is shown in self-effacement'.[50] Bishop Michael noted that it was the moral and spiritual appeal of *kenosis* that was important to Gore. God's love is His power, and that is why Jesus is the key to understanding how it prevails.

It is one thing to believe in the self-emptying of Christ and the self-restraint of God's love; it is another thing to make it the basis for priestly ministry and prophetic evangelism. But this Gore attempted; and Bishop Michael later followed in his footsteps. Gore's example as well as his learning gave him great moral authority in challenging the social injustices of his day, and in ensuring that a keen social conscience was central to Anglican Catholicism. Gore identified closely with the prophets in the Bible, those ambassadors for the living God, calling His people to repentance from their individual and social sins.

His belief in the living reality and moral demands of God also gave him confidence in upholding authority in the life of the Church, even at the risk of unpopularity and misunderstanding. Meanwhile Gore continued Newman's work on examining this vital issue, but within an Anglican context.[51] Reflecting on how Christ actually taught his disciples in the gospels, he built his own approach on the foundation laid by St Augustine, who said that 'authority is prior to reason in order of time, but reason is prior to authority in its essence'.[52] The authority of God is that of a Father educating His children; and Christ comes to unite human beings freely and lovingly, if at times painfully, to the Truth, which is himself, by the gift of his Spirit. Gore concluded that authority in the Church should never be 'irrational obedience, but instead intelligent correspondence with the divine purpose'.[53] Christian authority is something given away to enable others to function and to flourish. God's constant purpose is simply love: His truth revealed in Christ imparts freedom;[54] for as Jesus himself said: 'You will know the truth, and the truth will set you free.'[55]

Bishop Michael noted that when Gore came to examine Newman's doctrine of development, he asserted these criteria for discerning true development within the life and teaching

tradition of the Church: 'It must be open, accessible to the faithful at every stage, and susceptible of appeal to antiquity and
scripture by sound historical scholarship.'[56] This approach Gore
defined as that of 'Liberal Catholicism', anticipating in many
ways the spirit of Vatican II. He believed that it was the vocation
of Anglicanism to defend and develop it within the wider life
of Christendom. In protest at contemporary Roman Catholic
claims to infallibility, he declared: 'Revelation cannot be dimin-
ished or added to ... the later Church cannot know what the early
Church did not';[57] a principle that might also be applied within
Anglicanism to certain intellectual approaches to Christian tradition and morality, and to the critical study of the Bible. If there is
infallibility at the root of the Church's authority, it is found only
at the foot of the Cross. This is the place of ultimate truth for
human beings in their relationships with God and with each
other. Only here is the love of power and domination over others
overcome by the forgiving power of divine love. It is this power
alone, as Dante said, which moves the stars.[58]

✳ ✳ ✳

William Temple also exerted a decisive influence on Bishop
Michael's understanding of Christianity. Temple was one of the
towering spiritual leaders in the English church in the first half of
the twentieth century, especially between the two world wars,
and he served as Bishop of Manchester, Archbishop of York, and
briefly as Archbishop of Canterbury. As a Christian philosopher
and socialist, his influence reached far outside the orbit of the
Church and made a lasting impact on the life of the nation. At his
death in 1944 he was hailed by President Roosevelt as one of the
outstanding moral leaders in the English-speaking world.[59]

It was Bishop Michael's good fortune to have known Temple
personally as a young man. Their first encounter was during a
mission to the university of Cambridge in 1926. It was Temple's
fearless facing of the world and its complexities, and his deep
conviction about the importance of intellectual issues in theology,
which made the deepest impact upon Bishop Michael as a
student.[60] Temple later wrote to thank him for the publication in
1936 of his first book, *The Gospel and the Catholic Church*, and

shortly afterwards he invited him to join an ecumenical conference under his leadership at Bishopthorpe near York. A photograph of that meeting always hung on Bishop Michael's study wall.[61]

Throughout his life, Bishop Michael regarded Temple with a sort of holy hero worship, and asked to be buried near him in the cloisters of Canterbury Cathedral. Temple helped steer the appointment of him to the chair of theology at Durham, and Bishop Michael saw his own appointment as Archbishop of York as very much following in Temple's footsteps as a Christian thinker and writer within the life of the church.[62] Like many of his generation he felt that Temple's sudden death in 1944 robbed the Church of England of credible spiritual leadership for a crucial period immediately after the war.[63] His own ministry as a bishop and archbishop was guided by the memory of Temple's example, and he compared him as an archbishop to St Anselm.[64]

Bishop Michael paid close attention to Temple's theology and its influence in *From Gore to Temple*, and aspects of this have already been examined in this study. A major theme running throughout the book is how the debt Temple owed to Gore, and the significance of their differences, is crucial for understanding the development of Anglican theology between 1889 and 1939.[65] Temple published a book in 1924 entitled *Christus Veritas* in which he built upon Gore's vision of the incarnation as the key to the Christian understanding of the world, going on to portray it as the key also to the whole 'unity and rationality of a world whose every feature – evil and suffering included – must make sense'.[66] Temple criticized, however, the limitations of the theory of *kenosis*, which was so dear to Gore. He felt that it implied inconsistency in understanding the life of Jesus in the gospels, and made the incarnation a 'mere episode' in the life of God. Temple saw the incarnation instead as 'truly revealing and symbolic of God as He eternally is, showing us what God is ever and always like in the glory of His self-giving love'. He based his conviction upon his own profound understanding of St John's gospel.[67] Temple published his *Readings in St John's Gospel* between 1939 and 1945, and it proved to be one of his most popular and well-beloved books. Bishop Michael was never closer to the inner spirit of Temple's theology and spirituality than in his own devotion to and teaching about St John's gospel.

Bishop Michael reviewed the significance of Temple's approach to theology at the beginning of his concluding chapter in *From Gore to Temple*:

Temple's interest in particular doctrines was for the sake of their bearing upon theology proper, upon God Himself. Thus the kenotic question interested him less for what it suggests about the mode of the incarnation than for what it suggests about divine omnipotence and love. The atonement interested him not only for the sake of human salvation, but also for what he believed it to tell us of the sacrifice at the heart of the eternal God. Miracle, at which he had at one time stumbled, came to matter to him for his belief that God is personal. The visible Church was significant as the sacrament of eternity in the midst of time. ... For Temple, everything was related to God, and was to be cherished and studied in that relation.[68]

At the end of his discussion of Temple's theology, Bishop Michael drew attention to an important admission that Temple made as war broke out again in 1939. William Temple had consistently tried to explain to people in the Church and to English society the 'Christian map of life'. Now, however, he admitted serious if temporary defeat: 'The world of today is one of which no Christian map can be made. It must be changed by Christ into something very unlike itself before a Christian map is possible. We used to believe in the sovereignty of the God of love a great deal too light-heartedly.'[69] Temple noted that he now felt closer to the prophetic spirit of Gore's theology of redemption; and Bishop Michael concluded that 'nothing in his last years befitted his greatness more than the humility with which he acknowledged that his quest had failed, and that other tasks were superseding it'.[70]

* * *

Some of those tasks fell to Bishop Michael himself when he became Archbishop of Canterbury many years later, and some remain still to be resolved within the life of the Anglican and worldwide Church. He was adamant, however, that Anglicanism had great promise if only it would be true to itself, and remain united in its conviction about the gospel of Christ and its moral and social demands, and faithful to God's call to holiness, in the midst of its rich and worldwide diversity. Loyal to, and nurtured by, its own traditions of prayer and thought, it pointed beyond itself in all its imperfection to the hidden perfection of the one holy catholic and apostolic Church of God; and this was its historic spiritual vocation.

> For while the Anglican church is vindicated by its place in history, with a strikingly balanced witness to the gospel, to the Church and to sound learning, its greater vindication lies in pointing through its own history to something of which it is a fragment. Its credentials are its incompleteness, with the tension and travail in its soul. It is clumsy and untidy; it baffles neatness and logic. For it is sent not to commend itself as 'the best type of Christianity', but by its very brokenness to point to the universal Church wherein all have died.[71]

The strength of Anglicanism lies in its long and deep spiritual roots, stretching back over 1400 years, and embodied in its own tradition of saints and teachers to whom Bishop Michael felt that he owed so much. For if Lancelot Andrewes had inscribed as his episcopal motto the words: 'But who is sufficient for these things?' then Bishop Michael's message to his own church echoed other words of St Paul: 'What have you that you have not already received?' His life was laid down in the service of the gospel and the unity of the Church, and he communicated the truth of the vision captured in these words that are set above Bede's tomb in the Galilee chapel of Durham Cathedral:

> Christ is that Morning Star who, when the night of this world is past, brings to his saints the promised Light of Life and opens to them eternal day.[72]

Abbreviations

All texts are by Michael Ramsey

BS	*Be Still and Know*
CEA	*Canterbury Essays and Addresses*
CP	*The Christian Priest Today*
CTP	*Canterbury Pilgrim*
DA	*Durham Essays and Addresses*
FC	*The Future of the Christian Church*
FFF	*Freedom, Faith and the Future*
FM	*F.D. Maurice and the Conflicts of Modern Theology*
GC	*The Gospel and the Catholic Church*
GG	*The Glory of God and the Transfiguration of Christ*
GT	*From Gore to Temple*
GW	*God, Christ and the World*
HS	*The Holy Spirit*
IC	*Introducing the Christian Faith*
JP	*Jesus and the Living Past*
RC	*The Resurrection of Christ*
SS	*Sacred and Secular*

Bible references are generally from the Revised English Bible.

Notes

Notes to Chapter 1

1   Chadwick, O., *Michael Ramsey – A Life*, (Oxford) 1990, pp 32, 34
2   Hebrews 4:15
3   2 Corinthians 4:12
4   GC p 4
5   Romans 3:23
6   GC p 4
7   GC pp 6–7
8   Chadwick, *Michael Ramsey*, pp 41–2
9   GC p 10
10 GC p 12
11 St Mark 10:45
12 GC p 19
13 St John 12:24
14 GC p 18
15 GC p 21
16 GC p 21
17 GC pp 21–2
18 GC p 22
19 2 Corinthians 5:21
20 Hebrews 5:7–8
21 GC pp 22–3
22 Philippians 2:5–11
23 GC p 24
24 GC p 24
25 GC p 24
26 Revelation 13:8
27 GC p 25
28 GC p 26
29 Chadwick, *Michael Ramsey*, p 41
30 GC p 26
31 GC p 27
32 GC pp 29–30

33   GC p 30
34   GC p 33
35   GC p 38
36   GC p 38
37   1 Corinthians 6:19–20
38   GC p 39
39   GC p 39
40   GC p 40
41   GC p 41
42   GC p 42

Notes to Chapter 2

1   Revelation 13:8
2   GC p 125
3   Genesis 22:1–18
4   St John 3:16
5   GC p 114
6   GC p 122
7   St John 17:17–19
8   Hebrews 2:17–18
9   Hebrews 12:29
10   GC p 157 – St Augustine on Psalm 37
11   GC p 12
12   Hebrews 10:31
13   GC p 16
14   Zechariah 12:10
15   Revelation 1:7
16   St John 19:34–7
17   Cf. 1 John 5:6–12
18   St John 7:37–9
19   *The Christian Concept of Sacrifice*, Oxford: SLG Press, 1974
     (Chapter 6 in *Jesus and the Living Past*)
20   Cf. St Luke 2:22–4
21   *The Christian Concept of Sacrifice*, pp 3–4
22   Hebrews 9:14
23   *The Christian Concept of Sacrifice*, p 5
24   *The Christian Concept of Sacrifice*, p 6
25   *The Christian Concept of Sacrifice*, p 7
26   *The Book of Common Prayer*
27   Romans 12:1–2
28   St John 4:23–4
29   Cf. 1 Corinthians 15:35–44

30 RC pp 120–1
31 RC p 18 – 2 Corinthians 4:10
32 St Matthew 7:14
33 RC p 19
34 RC p 33
35 RC p 95
36 St John 16:20–1
37 St Luke 12:50
38 2 Corinthians 5:14
39 Galatians 4:19
40 Revelation 12:1–6
41 Romans 8:22
42 St John 17:17
43 GG p 78
44 GG p 87
45 GG p 85 – with a note citing St Gregory of Nyssa, *Oratio Catechetica Magna* XXIV
46 GT p 23
47 GT p 39
48 GT p 45
49 GT p 46
50 GT p 49
51 GT p 50
52 GT p 52 – *De Civitate Dei* X.20
53 GT p 58
54 Cf. GC pp 209–16 for an earlier discussion of Maurice's significance
55 FM p 22
56 St John 10:10
57 FM p 60 – citing Maurice's *Theological Essays*, 3rd edition, p 117
58 FM p 61
59 FM p 64
60 FM p 65
61 FM p 65
62 FM p 66
63 FM p 67
64 FM p 68
65 FM p 71
66 'Bruising the Serpent's Head: Father Benson and Atonement', in Smith, M. (ed.), *Benson of Cowley*, (Oxford) 1980 (here p 54) – citing a letter by Benson
67 Genesis 3:15
68 'Bruising the Serpent's Head', p 60

Notes to Chapter 3

1   Chadwick, *Michael Ramsey*, p 357
2   Chadwick, *Michael Ramsey*, p 365
3   JP p 61
4   JP p 57, discussing Romans 5:1–8
5   CTP p 68
6   CP pp 50–1
7   CP p 51
8   Chapter 4
9   CP p 22
10 CP p 23
11 St John 3:19
12 CP p 25
13 Chapter 10
14 CP p 48
15 Chapter 7
16 BS p 108
17 CP p 47
18 CP p 47
19 CP p 53
20 Hebrews 10:31
21 Hebrews 12:29
22 Hebrews 4:12–13
23 Chapter 7
24 St Mark 2:1–12
25 Letter to Eulogius, Archbishop of Alexandria in AD 598
26 CTP p 67
27 *The Simplicity of Prayer*, Oxford: SLG Press
28 Chapter 7
29 BS p 73
30 BS p 74
31 Chapter 3
32 CP p 13
33 Hebrews 7:25
34 CP p 14
35 CP pp 14–15
36 Psalm 46:10
37 CP p 17
38 CP p 18
39 CP p 14
40 Printed by SLG Press, Oxford
41 SS p 76
42 CTP p 158

43   *The Simplicity of Prayer*, Oxford
44   CTP p 127
45   CTP pp 137–8
46   CTP p 187

Notes to Chapter 4

1   1 Corinthians 4:7
2   GC p 44
3   GC p 45
4   GC pp 46 – 2 Corinthians 4:12
5   GC p 47
6   Galatians 3:28
7   GC p 49
8   GC p 60
9   GC p 66
10   GC p 89
11   GC p 93
12   GC p 101
13   GC p 103
14   GC p 107
15   2 Peter 1:4
16   Colossians 1:27
17   GC p 122
18   Psalm 36:9
19   GC p 126
20   Hebrews 13:8
21   GC p 139
22   St John 17:22
23   GG p 87
24   GG p 89
25   GG p 89
26   GG p 100
27   GG pp 133–4 – *Sermon* 51
28   GG p 134
29   GG p 139 – discussing Bulgakov's *Du Verbe Incarne*, (Paris) 1943
30   GG p 141 – citing Westcott in *The Historic Faith*, p 256
31   FFF p 38
32   FFF p 42
33   CTP p 7
34   CTP p 53
35   Chapter 11
36   BS p 113

37 BS p 114
38 BS p 116
39 *De Civitate Dei* XXII.30
40 BS p 123
41 SS p 15
42 SS p 18
43 SS p 21
44 SS p 20
45 SS p 24 – Hilary, *De Trinitate* II.2.4
46 SS p 25
47 SS p 26
48 St Augustine, *Confessions* X.38
49 SS p 37
50 SS pp 43–4 – St Gregory, *Moralia* XXX.8
51 SS p 71
52 GC pp 139–60
53 GC p 139 – Colossians 1:24
54 GC p 141
55 GC p 143 – St Athanasius, *De Incarnatione* 54
56 GC p 145 – St Cyril of Alexandria, on 1 John 5:2
57 GC pp 145–6 – St John Chrysostom, *Homily* XX on 1 Corinthians 9:10
58 GC p 147
59 GC p 150
60 GC p 151 – St Cyprian, *De Unitate* 4, 5
61 GC p 153 – St Augustine, *De Baptismo* III.21
62 GC p 155
63 GC p 156
64 GC p 158 – St Augustine, *Sermon* 272
65 GC p 159
66 GW p 115

Notes to Chapter 5

1 St John 16:13
2 Gore, C. (ed.), *Lux Mundi*, 1889, Chapter 8
3 Selwyn, E.G. (ed.), *Essays Catholic and Critical*, 1926, p vi
4 St Mark 12:30
5 CTP pp 79–81
6 Acts 2
7 HS p 131
8 HS p 7
9 HS p 9

10   HS p 15
11   HS p 25 – citing Dunn, J.G.D., *Jesus and the Spirit,* 1975, p 90
12   St Luke 10:21–2, cf. St Matthew 11:25–7
13   HS p 34
14   St John 10:10
15   HS p 59
16   HS pp 62–3
17   Romans 8:14–16, 26–8; HS p 66
18   HS p 76
19   1 Corinthians 6:19–20
20   1 Peter 2:9–10
21   HS p 80
22   HS p 81
23   St John 6:63
24   HS p 96
25   St John 16:14–15
26   St John 7:37–9
27   HS p 97
28   St John 3:16
29   Psalm 63:1
30   St Luke 2:35
31   St Mark 10:38–9
32   St John 19:34
33   St John 1:12
34   HS p 109
35   HS p 102
36   HS p 103
37   St John 20:22
38   HS p 110
39   HS p 120
40   HS pp 126–7
41   JP chapter 5
42   JP p 54
43   JP p 56
44   Galatians 2:20
45   JP p 59
46   Hebrews 13:8
47   GG p 6
48   GT chapter 9
49   'The Authority of the Bible', in Black, M. (ed.), *Peake's Commentary on the Bible,* 1962, p 1
50   'The Authority of the Bible', p 2
51   'The Authority of the Bible', p 3
52   'The Authority of the Bible', p 3

53 'The Authority of the Bible', p 4 – discussing the prologue to St John's Gospel
54 'The Authority of the Bible', p 5 – Origen, *De Principiis* 4.9
55 'The Authority of the Bible', p 5
56 'The Authority of the Bible', p 6
57 'The Authority of the Bible', p 7
58 Colossians 1:27
59 GC p 120
60 GC pp 124–5
61 GC p 126
62 RC – chapter three
63 RC p 35
64 RC p 36
65 RC p 40
66 RC p 41
67 RC p 120
68 GG p 20
69 GG p 24
70 GG p 30
71 GG p 31
72 GG p 33
73 GG p 62
74 GG p 67
75 GG p 75
76 GG p 86
77 Underhill, E., *Worship*, 1936, p 52
78 GG p 111
79 2 Corinthians 4:6
80 GG p 144
81 St John 6:63
82 St John 16:14–15
83 St John 4:24

Notes to Chapter 6

1 Chadwick, *Michael Ramsey*, p 195
2 Chadwick, *Michael Ramsey*, p 22
3 GC p 60
4 GC p 96
5 Chapter 8
6 GC p 99
7 GC p 101
8 GC p 103

9 1 Corinthians 10:16–22
10 GC pp 104–5
11 GC p 105
12 GC p 106
13 GC p 107
14 GC p 108
15 GC p 108
16 GC p 116 – discussing St Cyprian's teaching
17 St John 3:14–15
18 GC p 119
19 GG p 75
20 GG pp 76–7
21 St John 17:17
22 GG p 81
23 GT p 50
24 GT p 51
25 GT pp 52–3
26 GT p 115 – Gore's *The Incarnation of the Son of God*, 1898, p 218
27 GT p 158
28 GC pp 175–8
29 DA pp 18–19
30 DA p 19
31 DA p 21
32 DA p 21
33 CP p 10
34 CP p 16
35 GC p 89
36 GC p 90
37 GG p 91
38 GG p 93
39 CEA p 21
40 Cited in CEA p 22
41 CEA p 24
42 CEA p 26
43 CEA p 29
44 CEA p 30–1
45 St Augustine, *De Civitate Dei* XXII.30
46 CEA pp 32–40
47 CEA p 36
48 CEA p 40
49 St John 14:23
50 2 Corinthians 12:1–10
51 SS pp 32–3
52 SS p 33

53 SS p 36
54 SS p 37
55 SS pp 38–9
56 St Mark 15:34 – Jesus quoting the opening lines of Psalm 22
57 SS p 40
58 BS p 86
59 'The Mysticism of Evelyn Underhill', in Ramsey, A.M., and Allchin, A.M., *Evelyn Underhill – Anglican Mystic*, Oxford: SLG Press, 1996
60 'The Mysticism of Evelyn Underhill', p 5
61 'The Mysticism of Evelyn Underhill', p 13
62 'The Mysticism of Evelyn Underhill', p 14
63 Chadwick, *Michael Ramsey*, pp 317, 320
64 Chadwick, *Michael Ramsey*, pp 323–4
65 Chadwick, *Michael Ramsey*, pp 381, 390
66 CTP pp 87–90
67 CTP p 87
68 CTP p 88
69 CTP p 89
70 Cf. SS pp 42–4
71 DA pp 55–8
72 CEA pp 153–5
73 DA p 104
74 BS chapter 9
75 BS p 92
76 BS pp 93–4; cf. SS pp 37–8
77 BS p 94 – *The Cloud of Unknowing*, chapter 132
78 BS p 94
79 BS p 95
80 BS p 96
81 BS pp 97–8
82 BS pp 98–105
83 BS p 103
84 BS p 105
85 Allison Peers, E. (tr.), *The Living Flame of Love – St John of the Cross*, 1935/1977, p 77

Notes to Chapter 7

1 GC p 43
2 1 Corinthians 4:7
3 GC p 44
4 GC p 45
5 GC p 45

6   GC p 47 – again the debt to P.T. Forsyth is acknowledged
7   GC p 49
8   GC p 49 – from Barth, *Commentary on Romans*, (Oxford) 1933, p 396
9   GC pp 53–4
10   GC pp 55–6
11   GC p 57
12   GC p 59 – he claims support here from another Congregational
     theologian, H.T. Andrews
13   GC p 59
14   GC p 61
15   The influence of F.D. Maurice relates directly to this understanding
     of the creeds
16   GC p 62
17   GC p 63
18   Cf. GC pp 64–5
19   GC p 66
20   RC pp 89–90
21   RC p 92
22   RC p 93
23   RC p 95
24   RC p 96
25   RC p 97
26   Cf. GT pp 112–13
27   RC p 98
28   RC p 100
29   GG p 70
30   Cf. Ephesians 5:21f
31   GG p 72
32   GG p 74
33   Cf. GG p 77
34   GG pp 80–1
35   GG pp 97–9
36   Cf. GT p 115
37   CEA p 56
38   CEA p 55
39   CEA pp 56–7
40   CEA pp 57–8
41   CEA p 57
42   CEA p 58
43   CEA p 59
44   FC p 21
45   FC p 22
46   FC p 23
47   FC p 2

48   FC p 23
49   FC p 24
50   FC p 25
51   FC pp 26–7
52   FC p 27
53   FC pp 27–8
54   Chadwick, *Michael Ramsey*, pp 4, 23–6, 29, 35, 191–7
55   See Chadwick, *Michael Ramsey*, pp 341–6 for what follows
56   In Gill, R., and Kendall, L. (eds.), *Michael Ramsey as Theologian*,
     1995, p 80
57   GC p 213
58   GC p 215
59   FM pp 27–9
60   FM p 33
61   GT pp 127–8
62   Chadwick, *Michael Ramsey*, p 288; cf. p 390
63   Chadwick, *Michael Ramsey*, pp 289–312, has a full discussion of this
     aspect of his primacy
64   Chadwick, *Michael Ramsey*, p 310
65   A.M. Allchin, in Gill and Kendall (eds.), *Michael Ramsey as
     Theologian*, p 50
66   GC p 125
67   Allchin, in Gill and Kendall (eds.), *Michael Ramsey as Theologian*,
     p 56
68   GC p 147
69   GC p 148
70   GC pp 148–9
71   GC p 164
72   GC p 165
73   GC pp 178–9
74   Cf. Allchin's valuable discussion of a paper written by Ramsey in
     1946, in Gill and Kendall (eds.), *Michael Ramsey as Theologian*,
     pp 51–2
75   From the introduction to the translation of *Iconostasis*, written by
     Pavel Florensky, (New York) 1996, p 23
76   See Sophrony (Sakharov), Archimandrite, *Saint Silouan the Athonite*,
     (Essex) 1991
77   GG p 128
78   GG p 135
79   GG p 137
80   2 Peter 1:4
81   GG p 137
82   2 Corinthians 4:6
83   Cf. Romans 8:18–25

84   Cf. St John 1:14
85   GG p 146
86   CEA pp 60–1
87   CEA p 69
88   CEA p 70
89   CEA p 71 – citing again the words from St Hilary, *De Trinitate* II.2.4
90   CEA p 73
91   Cf. Chadwick's perceptive discussion of this, *Michael Ramsey*, pp 375–6
92   CEA p 30
93   BS p 76
94   Cf. L. Kendall's testimony in Gill and Kendall (eds.), *Michael Ramsey as Theologian*, p 136

Notes to Chapter 8

1   Chadwick, *Michael Ramsey*, p 41
2   From a letter to the Canterbury diocese in March, 1971; cited by Kendall, in Gill and Kendall (eds.), *Michael Ramsey as Theologian*, p 125
3   Kendall, in Gill and Kendall (eds.), *Michael Ramsey as Theologian*, p 136; from a diocesan letter of November 1965
4   FC pp 35–6
5   FC p 36
6   FC p 36
7   DA pp 23–4
8   DA p 24
9   DA p 26; cf. Hebrews 4:12
10 DA p 27
11 DA p 28
12 DA p 122
13 DA pp 128–9
14 CEA pp 156–7
15 CP p 88
16 CP p 91
17 CEA p 159
18 CEA p 160
19 CP p 4 – from P.T. Forsyth, *The Church and the Ministry*, 1917
20 CP p 4
21 CP p 90
22 St Matthew 5:1–12
23 CP p 6
24 CP p 93

25 2 Corinthians 5:20
26 CP p 9
27 2 Corinthians 2:16
28 CP pp 14–15
29 CP p 16
30 CP p 30
31 CP p 31
32 CP p 33; cf. Philippians 3:20–1
33 CP p 15
34 CP p 36
35 CP p 38
36 CP p 40
37 CP p 42
38 CP p 56, cf. 83
39 CP p 57
40 CP p 58
41 CP p 80
42 CP p 59
43 CP p 62
44 CP p 63
45 CP p 85
46 CP p 85
47 CP pp 64–5
48 CP p 77
49 CP p 67
50 CP p 70
51 CP p 91
52 CP pp 91–2
53 CP p 87
54 Chadwick, *Michael Ramsey*, pp 53–4
55 Chadwick, *Michael Ramsey*, p 95; cf. CEA pp 145–6
56 Chadwick, *Michael Ramsey*, pp 367–8
57 DA pp 106–9
58 DA p 108; cf. CEA p 155
59 CTP pp 65–6
60 CTP p 67
61 1 Thessalonians 5:17
62 CTP p 72
63 CTP p 67
64 CTP p 68
65 CP p 102
66 GC p 69
67 Cf. GC p 79
68 GC p 74

69   GC p 77
70   GC p 80
71   GC pp 82–3
72   GC Appendix II – 229–30: from an address to the convocation of
     Canterbury in May 1943
73   GC p 84
74   GC p 163; cf. Appendix I – 227–8
75   St Gregory the Great, *Letters* V.18, 43; VIII.30
76   GC p 65
77   GC Appendix I – 227–8
78   ARCIC, *The Final Report*, 1982
79   GC p 209
80   GC p 213
81   DA pp 87–8
82   DA p 96
83   CEA pp 161–2
84   CEA pp 165–6
85   CTP p 155
86   CP p 96
87   CP p 98
88   CP p 99
89   St Matthew 5:13
90   St John 21:18
91   CP p 93

Notes to Chapter 9

1   *The Alternative Service Book*, p 387
2   Chaucer, *The Canterbury Tales*, prologue – lines 477–528
3   Coleman, D. (ed.), *Michael Ramsey: The Anglican Spirit*, 1991, p 16
4   Coleman (ed.), *Michael Ramsey*, pp 18–19
5   Coleman (ed.), *Michael Ramsey*, p 21 (citing Hooker, *Of the Laws of
     Ecclesiastical Polity*, book V)
6   Coleman (ed.), *Michael Ramsey*
7   Coleman (ed.), *Michael Ramsey*, p 24
8   GC p 204
9   GC p 205 (citing Francis White's *Treatise of the Sabbath Day*, 1635)
10   GC p 206
11   GC p 206
12   Foreword to Lossky, N., *Lancelot Andrewes – The Preacher*,
     (Oxford) 1991
13   F.E. Brightman's introduction to the *Preces Privatae*, p xxix
14   *Preces Privatae*, p xxxiii

15 *Preces Privatae*, p xxxiv

16 *Preces Privatae*, p xxxv

17 *Preces Privatae*, p xxxviii

18 Brightman's judgement, endorsed by G.M. Story, in Story, G.M. (ed.), *Lancelot Andrewes: Sermons*, (Oxford) 1967, p xlviii

19 N. Lossky's conclusion to *Lancelot Andrewes*, p 326–7 for what follows

20 Lossky, *Lancelot Andrewes*, pp 328–9

21 Lossky, *Lancelot Andrewes*, p 331

22 Lossky, *Lancelot Andrewes*, p 333

23 Lossky, *Lancelot Andrewes*, p 341

24 Lossky, *Lancelot Andrewes*, p 345

25 Lossky, *Lancelot Andrewes*, p 351; cf. Evagrius of Pontus, 'Treatise on Prayer: 153 texts', in the *Philokalia*, vol I (1979), p 62 – text 61

26 Lossky, *Lancelot Andrewes*, pp 351–2; Newman himself translated the *Preces Privatae* in Tract 88 (1840)

27 CEA p 114

28 CEA pp 112–15 for what follows

29 Coleman (ed.), *Michael Ramsey*, p 64

30 Coleman (ed.), *Michael Ramsey*, p 53

31 Chadwick, *Michael Ramsey*, p 22

32 Chadwick, *Michael Ramsey*, p 93

33 Chadwick, *Michael Ramsey*, pp 27–9; note Ramsey's tribute to him in his foreword to Wakefield, G. (ed.), *Crucifixion-Resurrection*, 1981, xi-xii

34 See Chadwick, O., *The Founding of Cuddesdon*, (Oxford) 1954

35 Newton, J.A., *Search for a Saint: Edward King*, 1977, p 44

36 Newton, *Search for a Saint*, p 51

37 Newton, *Search for a Saint*, p 60

38 Newton, *Search for a Saint*, p 74

39 See Russell, G.W.E., *Edward King – Bishop of Lincoln* and more recently by Newton, *Search for a Saint*

40 Newton, *Search for a Saint*, p 105

41 Newton, *Search for a Saint*, p 120 – 2 Samuel 22:36; cf. Psalm 18:35 (AV)

42 Carpenter, J., *Gore: A Study in Liberal Catholic Theology*, p 9. n. 11

43 GT p 4 – citing A. Moore in Gore (ed.), *Lux Mundi*, p 99

44 GT p 23

45 Carpenter, *Gore*, p 143

46 Gore, C., *Belief in God*, p 173 – cited by Carpenter, *Gore*, p 112

47 Gore, C., *Can We Then Believe?*, pp 76–8 – cited by Carpenter, *Gore*, p 155; cf. GT pp 16–17

48 GT p 21

49 GT pp 30–1

50 GT p 34
51 See Carpenter, *Gore*, chapter 5
52 Carpenter, *Gore*, p 119
53 Gore, C., *Our Place in Christendom*, p 172; cited by Carpenter, *Gore*, p 119
54 Cf. Gore (ed.), *Lux Mundi*, p 237; cf. GT p 98
55 St John 8:32
56 GT p 99
57 Gore, C., *Roman Catholic Claims*, pp 37, 42; cited by Carpenter, *Gore*, p 124
58 Dante, *Divina Commedia – Inferno*, Canto I, lines 38–40
59 Iremonger, F.A., *William Temple, Archbishop of Canterbury*, (Oxford) 1948, p 627
60 Chadwick, *Michael Ramsey*, p 25
61 Chadwick, *Michael Ramsey*, pp 49–51
62 Chadwick, *Michael Ramsey*, pp 56, 89–90
63 Chadwick, *Michael Ramsey*, p 373
64 GT p 160
65 GT p vii
66 GT p 24; he discusses also L. Thornton's *The Incarnate Lord* (1928); cf. CEA pp 127–32
67 GT p 41; Temple was, however, challenged by O. Quick, Ramsey's predecessor at Durham
68 GT pp 146–7
69 GT pp 160–1
70 GT pp 160–1
71 GC p 220
72 From Bede's *Commentary on the Apocalypse*

Select Bibliography

(Place of publication London unless stated otherwise)

PUBLISHED WORKS BY MICHAEL RAMSEY

The Gospel and the Catholic Church, 1936/1956, reprinted 1990
The Significance of Anglican-Orthodox Relations, (Sobornost) 1938
The Resurrection of Christ, 1945, revised edition, 1961
'What is Anglican Theology?', *Theology*, 1945
The Church of England and the Eastern Orthodox Church: Why their Unity is Important, 1946
The Glory of God and the Transfiguration of Christ, 1949, revised edition, 1967
F.D. Maurice and the Conflicts of Modern Theology, 1951
Charles Gore and Anglican Theology, 1955
Durham Essays and Addresses, 1956
From Gore to Temple: The Development of Anglican Theology between 'Lux Mundi' and the Second World War 1889–1939, 1960
Introducing the Christian Faith, 1961
'The Authority of the Bible', in Black, M. (ed.), *Peake's Commentary on the Bible*, 1962
Image Old and New, 1963
Canterbury Essays and Addresses, 1964
The Meaning of Prayer, 1964
Sacred and Secular, 1965
Jesus the Living Lord, 1966 (Oxford: SLG Press, 1992)
Problems of Christian Belief, London: BBC Publications, 1966
Rome and Canterbury, 1967
God, Christ and the World: A Study in Contemporary Theology, 1969
Freedom, Faith and the Future, 1970
The Future of the Christian Church, 1971
The Christian Priest Today, 1972, revised edition 1985
The Charismatic Christ, 1974
Canterbury Pilgrim, 1974
The Christian Concept of Sacrifice, Oxford: SLG Press, 1974

'The Mysticism of Evelyn Underhill', 1975 (in Ramsey, A.M., and Allchin, A.M., *Evelyn Underhill – Anglican Mystic*, Oxford: SLG Press, 1996)
Come Holy Spirit, (New York) 1976
The Holy Spirit, 1977
Jesus and the Living Past, (Oxford) 1980
Lent with St John, 1980
Be Still and Know, 1982

Works by Other Authors

Allchin, A.M., *The Silent Rebellion: Anglican Religious Communities 1845–1900*, 1958
—— *The Dynamic of Tradition*, 1981
—— *The World is a Wedding*, 1978
—— *The Kingdom of Knowledge and Love*, 1979
—— *The Joy of All Creation*, 1984
—— *Participation in God*, 1988
Allison Peers, E. (tr.) *The Living Flame of Love – St John of the Cross*, 1935/1977
Andrewes, Lancelot, *Preces Privatae*, ed. F.E. Brightman, 1903
ARCIC, *The Final Report*, 1982
Baker, J.A., *The Foolishness of God*, 1970
Baillie, D.M., *God Was in Christ*, 1948
Barrington-Ward, S., *The Jesus Prayer*, (Oxford) 1996
Barth, K., *Commentary on Romans*, (Oxford) 1933
Bouyer, L., *A History of Christian Spirituality*, Vol. 3, 1968
Burnaby, J., *Amor Dei*, 1938
—— *The Belief of Christendom*, 1959
Carpenter, J., *Gore: A Study in Liberal Catholic Theology*, 1960
Chadwick, O., *The Founding of Cuddesdon*, (Oxford) 1954
—— *The Mind of the Oxford Movement*, 1960, third edition, 1971
—— *Michael Ramsey – A Life*, (Oxford) 1990
Church, R.W., *The Oxford Movement*, (Chicago) 1970
Clare, Mother Mary, *Encountering the Depths*, 1981
Clement, O., *On Being Human – A Spiritual Anthology*, (New York) 2000
Coleman, D. (ed.), *Michael Ramsey: The Anglican Spirit*, 1991
Curtis, G., *William of Glasshampton*, 1947
Dales, D.J., *Living through Dying – The Spiritual Experience of St Paul*, (Cambridge) 1993
Dix, G., *The Shape of the Liturgy*, 1945
Duggan, M., *Through the Year with Michael Ramsey*, 1975
Dunn, J.G.D., *Jesus and the Spirit*, 1975

Florensky, P., *Iconostasis*, (New York) 1996

Forsyth, P.T., *The Church and the Ministry*, 1917

Gill, R., and Kendall, L. (eds.), *Michael Ramsey as Theologian*, 1995

Gore, C. (ed.), *Lux Mundi*, 1889

—— *The Incarnation of the Son of God*, 1898

—— *The Body of Christ*, 1901

—— *The Reconstruction of Belief*, 1926

—— *Can We Then Believe?*, 1926

Hastings, A., *A History of English Christianity 1920–1985*, second edition, 1987

Hooker, R., *Of the Laws of Ecclesiastical Polity*, 1907, repr. 1965

Iremonger, F.A., *William Temple, Archbishop of Canterbury*, (Oxford) 1948

Kendall, L., *Gateway to God – Daily Readings with Michael Ramsey*, 1988

—— *The Mind in the Heart – Michael Ramsey: Theologian and Man of Prayer*, Oxford: SLG Press, 1991

Ker, I., *Newman and the Fullness of Christianity*, (Edinburgh) 1993

—— *Healing the Wound of Humanity – The Spirituality of John Henry Newman*, 1993

Kirk, K.E., *The Vision of God*, 1931

Lloyd, R., *The Church of England 1900–1965*, 1966

Lossky, N., *Lancelot Andrewes – The Preacher*, (Oxford) 1991

Lossky, V., *The Mystical Theology of the Eastern Church*, 1957

—— *The Vision of God*, 1963

—— *In the Image and Likeness of God*, 1975

Loyer, O., *L'Anglicanisme de Richard Hooker*, (Paris) 1979

McAdoo, H.R., *The Spirit of Anglicanism*, 1965

Mascall, E.L., *He who Is – A Study in Traditional Theism*, 1943

Milner-White, E., *My God, My Glory*, 1954

Moberly, R.C., *Ministerial Priesthood*, 1897

—— *Atonement and Personality*, 1901

More, P.E., and Cross, F.L. (eds.), *Anglicanism*, 1962

Moorman, J.R.H., *A History of the Church of England*, 1953

Newton, J.A., *Search for a Saint: Edward King*, 1977

Pawley, B. and Pawley, M., *Rome and Canterbury through Four Centuries*, 1981

Prestige, G.L., *Life of Charles Gore*, 1935

Quick, O.C., *Doctrines of the Creed*, 1938

Rowell, G., *The Vision Glorious*, (Oxford) 1983

—— *et. al.* (eds.) *Love's Redeeming Work is Done*, (Oxford) 2001

Russell, G.W.E., *Edward King – Bishop of Lincoln*, 1913

Selwyn, E.G. (ed.), *Essays Catholic and Critical*, 1926

Smith, B.A., *Dean Church, the Anglican Response to Newman*, 1958

Smith, M. (ed.), *Benson of Cowley*, (Oxford) 1980

Sophrony (Sakharov), Archimandrite, *Saint Silouan the Athonite*, (Essex) 1991

—— *Prayer*, (Essex) 1996

Southern, R.W., *St Anselm – A Portrait in a Landscape*, (Cambridge) 1990

Story, G.M. (ed.), *Lancelot Andrewes: Sermons*, (Oxford) 1967

Sykes, S.W., *The Integrity of Anglicanism*, 1978

—— *et. al.*, *The Study of Anglicanism*, revised edition, 1998

Temple, W., *Christus Veritas*, 1924

—— *Nature, Man and God*, 1934

—— *Readings in St John's Gospel*, 1945

Thornton, L., *The Incarnate Lord*, 1928

Underhill, E., *Worship*, 1936

Von Hügel, F., *The Mystical Element of Religion*, 1908

—— *Essays and Addresses on the Philosophy of Religion*, 1924

Wakefield, G. (ed.), *Crucifixion-Resurrection*, 1981

—— 'Michael Ramsey: A Theological Appraisal', *Theology*, November 1988

Ward, B., *The Prayers and Meditations of St Anselm*, 1973

Ware, K., *The Orthodox Church*, 1963

—— *The Power of the Name – The Jesus Prayer in Orthodox Spirituality*, Oxford: SLG Press, 1974

Welsby, P.A., *A History of the Church of England 1945–1980*, (Oxford) 1984

Westcott, B.F., *The Gospel of St John*, 1892

Williams, R. (ed.), *Sergii Bulgakov – Towards a Russian Political Theology*, (Edinburgh) 1999

Index of Biblical Quotations

Index of Names